Canto Divina
Singing Psalms for Transformation

Written by Deborah Ann Keefe, MSW
August 15th, 2020

ISBN 978-1-7333199-6-6

Published 2021
All scripture quotations are taken from the Revised Standard Version of the Bible,
Second Catholic Edition.

Dedication

This book is dedicated to my daughters,
Naomi and Abigail Keefe.
Thank you for teaching me what love is all about.

My love for you is boundless...

Contents

Foreword

By Mike Aquilina

Some years ago I wrote a little book titled *How the Choir Converted the World: Through Hymns, With Hymns, In Hymns*. Its thesis was simple: Music was the ordinary means by which the early Church reached the hearts and minds of believers. As St. Basil the Great noted in the fourth century, Christians might tune out a sermon and even forget the Scripture readings at Mass. But they could not help but remember the Psalms they sang. The melodies made them unforgettable. They walked home whistling the tune and, inevitably, thinking about the words.

In an age when literacy was rare, music was perhaps the most important way the Church catechized its people. It was the most effective delivery system for doctrine. The earworm arrived at Mass — and it stayed, repeatedly delivering the message whenever the tune came to mind.

Thus, when heretics attacked the tenets of the faith, the great teachers of antiquity responded not only with learned theological treatises. They also composed hymns. Men like St. Ambrose of Milan and St. Hilary of Poitiers established the custom of dedicating a final verse, a "doxology," to praise of the undivided Trinity. They did this in order to overcome the Arian heresy, and it worked.

For Christians, music has always served as a teacher, a guide, and a healer. In his memoirs, St. Augustine described how after his mother's death he worked through his grief by singing her favorite hymns.

It was music, in a sense, that converted the world to Christ. Music evangelized generations of stubborn, sinful people. And evangelization is what we're supposed to be doing today. For a half-century now, our popes have urged us to carry out a "new evangelization. They've made clear, moreover, that this task is not reserved to a special class of professionals. It's not the job of the clergy or people with prestigious degrees. It is universal and non-optional. Pope St. John Paul II spoke of "the universal call to holiness and apostolate." So it's part of the basic Christian package: If we're baptized, we have a duty to evangelize. And it would be worthwhile for us to imitate our ancestors in the faith, applying music as we respond to our vocation — sharing music in order to heal, instruct, and guide our friends and neighbors.

Musicians should be especially keen to do this. Yet it's not just for musicians. Music is integral to lives today in different ways. We give CDs as gifts and replicate our listening experiences. We share playlists on streaming services. We post videos on social media. These are ways we can do for our time what Ambrose and Hilary did for theirs. Evangelization is so important, and music should be front and center in our efforts.

Yet there is something even more basic than evangelization. In fact, it is a pre-condition of evangelization. The 19th-century spiritual writer Dom Jean-Baptiste Chautard called it the "soul of the apostolate", and the soul of the apostolate is prayer.

We need to pray in the first place. We need to pray without ceasing. We need to draw close to the heart of Jesus and intercede with him for others. Yet even our prayer — like our proclamation of the Gospel — can be enhanced by music.

That is the consensus of Christian tradition. And it's the genius of Deborah Ann Keefe's book. In these pages, she draws from the ancient sources, as well as modern disciplines and personal experiences, as she proposes a thoroughly Christian program for healing — physical, psychological, moral, and spiritual healing. Its keynotes are the Psalms, the songs of ancient Israel that the Church took to the world. They are perfect prayers, reflecting the full range of human emotion and need. They convey it all in vivid poetry, which we put to memorable melody, because we need to remember.

Begun in prayer, in the soul of the apostolate, this book is a heartfelt work of evangelization — an extension of Jesus' healing to a world in need.

There is only so much that can be credibly said *about* music, and I have probably exceeded that word count by now. The proof is in the singing and the hearing. And now it begins.

Acknowledgments

I have been very blessed to live a life according to Catholic values. I have always felt the love of God in my heart calling me to be all that He created me to be. God, family, friends, and service to others guide me each day. I have been blessed with loving and educating two exceptional children, performing with two orchestras, and teaching flute to public, private, charter, and home- educated students. I have also been blessed to research and develop the application of music as medicine in the field of social work. My life has been centered on building and supporting the health and wellness of families through faith, education, and music.

I would like to thank my daughters, Naomi and Abigail Keefe, for inspiring me to follow my dream. As a family they are my "Dream Team", always wanting what is best for each of us. We build each other up with loving support and encouragement. All things are possible with Jesus Christ leading the way.

I would like to thank Mike Aquilina for understanding the importance of this work and helping me to see it through the publishing process. Thank you, Mike, for leading the way and inspiring me to reach for new heights.

I would like to thank Meryl Kaleida for copyediting this work and supporting me through the journey of becoming an author. Your attention to details, insightful comments, and guidance have brought *Canto Divina* to a new level.

I would like to thank the Hochreiter and St. Pierre families for blessing my children and me with your abundant love and grace. Truly, you are a living testament to our faith.

I would like to thank Harriet and her family for believing in me and the importance of this work. Harriet has spent countless hours revealing the Eucharistic love of Jesus Christ to me so that I can share this work with all of you. Her love for Our Blessed Mother and surrender to the Divine Will of Christ inspires me to lead with dignity, grace, and strength.

I would like to thank John and Diane Barton and family for teaching me the courage to face each new day with faith and hope in Our Lord Jesus Christ, the Sacraments of our One Holy, Catholic and Apostolic Church, and Adoration.

I would like to thank Johnny Bertucci and the Ark and the Dove in Pittsburgh, PA. Praise God for a New Pentecost!!! Thank you for believing in me and my work. Thank you for blessing me with the gift of Matthew Bourgeois and Charis Publishing. *Veni Sancte Spiritus!*

I would like to thank Father Daniel Scheidt, pastor of Saint Vincent De Paul Catholic Parish in Fort Wayne, Indiana. Truly, his love for God and leadership of the Church through a time of transformation is inspiring! Thank you for planting the seeds for *Canto Divina* and believing in me and my work.

I would like to thank Father Greg Bramlage, Angie, David, Ann and the Missionaries of the New Evangelization. Hallelujah! Christ is King! Thank you for stepping into the front lines with Jesus and claiming His victory here on earth.

I would like to thank Father John Broussard, rector of Our Lady of Good Help in Champion, Wisconsin. His spiritual direction for my personal transformation and this work was truly from God. Thank you for teaching me how to surrender my life to Jesus and place it on His altar. Thank you for showing me the love and mercy of Christ.

Thank you for all my friends at Our Lady of Good Help who prayed for me: Don, Lisa, Petrine, Annie, David, Peggy, and Bob. Thank you for sharing so many beautiful Rosary processions with me guided by the love, comfort, and strength of Our Blessed Mother.

Thank you to Father Jim Jugenheimer and Saint Pius X Parish. Thank you for welcoming me and blessing me with your lovely Perpetual Adoration Chapel. Thank you, Dr. Robin Goldsmith, for seeing and believing in my soul as I walked through the darkness. God is good!

I would like to thank the Guyette family, the Proulx family, the Allegretti family, the McGunagle family, the Horton family, and the Walker family for shepherding me in the storm. Yes, God is Love.

Introduction

This book has been written in the presence of the Holy Eucharist, in Adoration chapels across the country. As I surrendered my will and my work to the divine will of God, I remained immersed in the sacraments of the Catholic Church. In order to share my faith, education, and cultural perspective, I offer you the following experiences in my life that influenced this work.

We all know the importance of building relationships and making connections in our lives. The advent of social media has radically changed the manner in which we connect to others and the speed to which we do so. Google searches, Apple apps, and instant messaging continue to offer a world in which connections are made instantaneously. You can find research and applications on a multitude of subjects without leaving the sanctuary of your home. There is no longer a pause before we ask someone to "be our friend", we just click a button and send a request. We are valued today by how many connections we have, without considering the quality of them at all.

Facebook and Instagram lead the way with individuals posting pictures of themselves, their families, and all their activities. It has been said that a picture says a thousand words. Yes, that is true, however, a picture is only a snapshot of a moment in time: pictures do not tell the whole story. Given the appropriate tools and techniques, anyone can look good in a picture, the real question is, what is the whole story? Do we care about what really happened, or do we make snap judgments about people's lives based on a snapshot? To know someone, to love them, to care for them, takes time. Just ask a dying patient what they would like most of all, most would answer, "Time with the people they love." You cannot buy time, and you cannot get it back once it is gone. The only thing that lasts forever is LOVE. Love takes time to develop but lasts for eternity.

I remember when I knelt down at my father's open coffin. He had died suddenly of a massive heart attack in the middle of the night. Unfortunately, he had hit his head and the mark it left was still very visible. I pondered his last moments and wished I could have been there to catch him when he fell, to hold his hand, to take away his suffering. My father and I were blessed with the spirit of love and forgiveness. As I knelt before him, I was recently divorced, questioning my faith, and knew my father understood my suffering. In a holy moment, God guided me to put my hand on my father's heart. It was a moment I will never forget. His heart was warm. It radiated his love for me. My father had passed away one week prior, and his heart was still warm. I felt his love for me and knew it would never end. This was his last gift to me here on earth, and I praised God for this miracle. I could feel my father's love through God's love for me. It was like picking the petals off a daisy and reciting, "He loves me, He loves me not, He loves me, He loves me not, He loves me, He loves me not," and finding the answer to be, "HE LOVES ME!" Yes, love never ends.

My faith life was formed at Notre Dame Parish in New Hyde Park, New York where my parents were active members of the church. My father taught drum and bugle corps, and my mother taught CCD. My father's faith was evident in his commitment to Catholicism under all circumstances. My mother's faith reflected the joy of the Resurrection. Thank God for my grandmother, Mary, who was devoted to Catholicism and prayed many Rosaries for our family.

The most joyful time of year in my family was Easter. My mother would take us shopping for Easter dresses, bonnets, shoes, purses, and gloves with a sense of determination and lightness of her soul. We had survived another cold winter, and the tulips were displaying their brilliant colors after being covered with snow. My mother always pointed out this miracle of spring while singing her favorite song:

> *I am the resurrection and the life*
> *He who believes in me*
> *Will live a new life*
>
> *I have come to bring you life*
> *I have come to bring you hope*
> *If you believe*
> *Then you shall live*

My mother was more an artist than a musician and, honestly, this is the only song I remember her singing. I have been told that it is a very anointed song, and I believe it is. My mother always focused on the Resurrection of Jesus Christ and new life. Her joy during this season would infiltrate my heart and lead me to a lifelong love of flowers, faith, and song.

Sometimes I wonder what our Catholic faith would look like if we focused more on the Resurrection than on the

Crucifixion. Truly, Jesus was victorious over all sin and death and would want us to claim His victory in our life. I wonder if we taught children about the love and forgiveness of Christ first and waited to teach them about His Crucifixion until they were old enough to process this information, if more of our children would remain Catholic in their adult lives.

One of the lessons I enjoyed teaching during a Vacation Bible School program relates the gift of focusing on the love and forgiveness of Jesus Christ. The Gospel lesson was from Matthew 3:1-17, "The Preaching of John the Baptist" and "The Baptism of Jesus". One of my favorite lines from this Scripture is, "Prepare the way of the Lord, make his paths straight." I hoped that the exercise would help me bring the children the love and forgiveness of Christ so that they would follow Him always.

I began with a clean white linen sheet and a black marker. We made the sign of the cross, and I reminded the children that they were real sons and daughters of a Mighty King. We belonged to Him, and He had something to teach us today, so we must be still and listen. Yes, God is the only "perfect" in the world and by learning about Him we could become more like Him. It was also important to understand that God is "perfect", 100% pure and holy, and that our job was to become more and more like Him every day. Since we are not God, we could never be 100% pure and holy, but we could live our lives moving in this direction. Each day we would face choices to be more like Him or less like Him.

When we made choices that drew us away from God, we separated ourselves from Him. This was called sin. Sometimes I remember sin as the acronym "Saying an Inside No" to God. Some of the examples I shared were not doing my homework, forgetting my chores, staying angry at my sister, and not helping my neighbor. As I carefully made the room safe to admit our sins, I suggested I write them down on the sheet. As the children shared, (about seventy-five elementary school students), the sheet became more black than white. I could see the growing concern about what we would do with the sheet when we were done. I continued to write.

The more I wrote, the more I noticed the look of concern spreading across the room. There were sighs of relief as we began to share the burden of sin, but there was also a growing tension that you could touch and feel with your fingertips. I decided to engage the class in the solution.

I looked at them and said, "What should we do with this now?" Silence. I thought for a minute about what I had done with these sins. I put the sheet on the floor below me and I stomped my feet on it saying, "Oh, I am so bad, I did it again! No one will ever love me!" The children connected. There was a sadness on their faces that I will never forget. Perhaps I was not alone in this battle to accept God's love for me. Next, I tossed the sheet into the crowd and said, "They did it! They hurt me! They are bad! It's all their fault!" No one wanted the sheet. It quickly returned to me like a "hot potato". I took the sheet and wrapped it around myself whimpering, "I am bad, it is all my fault, no one loves me, I am unlovable." You could hear a pin drop. "Be still and know I am God" echoed in my heart. Please Lord, let them feel Your love for them.

Then, Betsy, our VBS Director, entered the room. She was carrying a pitcher of water. Betsy invited me to her table. She was filled with light, and I was drawn to her presence. I looked at the children, and their eyes told me to go to Betsy's table. I did. We stood next to each other, Betsy with the water and me with the sheet of sin. How could I ever be friends with her? We were opposites. She was good, and I was bad. Surely, Jesus could see this. But then Betsy asked me if I was willing to give my sins to Jesus, to be forgiven. She would not force me to give away my sins, she simply asked and gave me the choice of what I would do with my sins. Her radiance called to me. I wanted to feel better; I wanted what she had. I was tired of being filled with sin. I looked at the children and asked them, "Should I let Jesus take away my sins? Should I try whatever Betsy is offering me at her table?" It was a resounding, "YES!" There was no other option. I looked at Betsy and said, "Yes, I am willing to give my sins to Jesus and receive His forgiveness. What do I need to do with this sheet now?" She smiled and asked me to take one end of the sheet while she took the other. We held it over a large basin. It was time for the pitcher of water. I am usually an optimistic person, but I just could not imagine a way for God to take away these sins! I wrote them in a thick, black magic marker! I panicked; Betsy smiled. She was the VBS Director after all.

Betsy began to pour the water over the sheet and a hush filled the room. The sins were literally being washed away! Yes, one at a time the black ink was slowly finding its way down the white sheet in the large basin. The sheet had been filled with black sins, and I never imagined we would see the white sheet rise again. It took some time, but within five minutes the sins were all washed away, and the sheet was completely white again. By this time, the children were cheering and shouting, "Alleluia! It is a miracle! Jesus is AWESOME!!!" Honestly, I could not stop the tears from flowing. Do not ever doubt the power of God to be victorious in any situation. The children learned about the love AND forgiveness of God!

How could we not be happy? How could we not be grateful? God loved us so much He would take away our sins, forgive us, and love us back to wholeness so that we might go out and share the Good News with others! (Just don't forget to bring your water-soluble black marker.)

Today I realize that, despite my mother's many challenges, her gift to me of living in the joy of the Resurrection is priceless. Truly, when Jesus comes back to life on Easter morning, His first words are, "Peace be with you" (Jn 20:19). He follows with, "Peace be with you. As the Father has sent me, even so I send you" (Jn 20:21). He finishes by breathing on them and saying, "Receive the Holy Spirit. If you forgive the sins of any, they are forgiven; if you retain the sins of any, they are retained" (Jn 20:22-23). He is not angry, bitter, or resentful. Jesus is loving and forgiving and will never leave us.

We are not abandoned. Indeed, He breathes on us and gives us the gift of the Holy Spirit, our Advocate. We will never be separated from His love again. I believe it is much easier to believe in Jesus Christ if we understand His love and forgiveness. Like the mustard seed, my belief in Jesus Christ and my hope for a new life has blessed me with resilience, courage, and perseverance in the midst of the storms of life. What happened in between the Crucifixion and the Resurrection? Love and forgiveness.

As my spiritual life continued into adulthood, I continued to seek out the nature of God. My favorite hymn growing up in the Catholic Church was, "The King of Glory":

The King of Glory comes
The Nation rejoices
Open the gates before him
Lift up your voices

Who is the King of Glory?
What shall we call him?
He is Immanuel
The promised of ages

In all of Galilee
In city or village
He goes among his people
Curing their illness
Sing then of David's Son
Our savior and brother
In all of Galilee
Was never another

He gave his life for us
The Lamb of Salvation
He took upon himself
The sins of a Nation

He conquered sin and death
He truly has risen
And he will share with us
His heavenly vision

Canto Divina xxii

My childhood image of this "King of Glory" returned to me when I was a member of the Covenant Contemporary Worship Group at Saint Marie Parish in Manchester, New Hampshire. When I heard our gifted tenor singing this hymn it brought peace to my soul. Was it the words? I recalled the John's Gospel which begins with, "In the beginning was the Word, and the Word was with God, and the Word was God" (Jn 1:1). Was it the love in the singer's heart resonating through the music? Certainly, my soul was healing with the sound of his voice. Was it the confidence and power that he projected for all to see? I could see and hear Jesus in him.

This song also reminds me of the "Litany of the Divine Attributes", written by Mother Angelica. It is the most beautiful declaration of the nature and glory of God that I have ever read. Here are some of the highlights:

Divine Immensity that fills and contains all things.
Response: Possess me through and through that I may be all things to all men.

Divine Mercy infinite and without measure.
Response: Let me forgive and forget with love and compassion.

Divine Peace, ever tranquil and serene in the midst of turmoil.
Response: Let me maintain a quiet spirit and be strong enough to accept adversities with peace.

Divine Joy who alone art the source of all happiness.
Response: Give me that joy that no man can take away from me.

Divine Justice, who judges everything in the light of truth through the eyes of mercy.
Response: Grant that I may not judge my neighbor's motives, but give him the benefit of the doubt.

Divine Immutability, ever the same and never changing.
Response: Make my vacillating will stronger that I may not stray from the path of holiness.

Divine Omnipresence, behind me, before me, and around me.
Response: Let me see Your Face in everything so that all Your creation may speak to me of Your beauty.

Divine Compassion, so patient and understanding.
Response: Let me be sympathetic with my neighbor's needs and give him my love as well as my deeds.

(Mother Angelica on God, His Home, and His Angels, 73-75)

Perhaps, Mother Angelica's knowledge of and experience with the true nature of God was her strength during her many times of trials. When we know who God is, and therefore who we are in Him, nothing can stop us. We walk forward, one day at a time, with peace, love, joy, and compassion.

As I continued to be drawn to the glory and splendor of Jesus Christ, I was blessed with visiting the National Shrine of the Immaculate Conception in Washington, D.C. I will never forget the holy moment when I came upon the magnificent painting of Jesus Christ rising above the altar. He is adorned with a royal red robe, and His muscular arms are raised above Him. He has a fierce look of determination upon His face. Surely, I had found the King of Glory and He would win the battle for our nation.

As I explored this beautiful shrine and wondered what my part in God's plan of restoration was, I was met by the sound of "angels" singing Gregorian Chant. Yes, the Choir of the Basilica was rehearsing in a chapel below the sanctuary surrounded by portraits of the saints. Their voices called to me, and I was completely mesmerized by the purity and unity of their sound. It was as if I stepped into Heaven with a choir of angels praising God for all His glory and splendor. I heard God whisper to me, "Teach them to sing." In a holy moment, I responded, "Yes, Lord, I will teach them to sing!"

A Musician's Life

My musical life began when I was 2 years old, when my grandfather gave me a toy xylophone for Christmas and spent hours teaching me to play it. I found such joy in creating music with him! My next instrument was the accordion. Our family celebrated Sunday dinners at an Italian restaurant after Mass each week, and there was an accordion player who would come to each table to sing and play. We would sing along with him and this was a wonderful time of love and connection for my family, and I treasured each moment. There was something about the music that seemed to unite us.

I still remember the diamond middle C on the left hand and the piano keyboard on the right. The coordination needed to perform the "Um Pa Pas" with the chords on the left, play the melody on the right, while moving the bellows in and out to produce the sound, is truly extraordinary. All three aspects are needed to play songs for an audience, with the air moving through the bellows as the connector. I picked it up quickly and enjoyed learning new music and being able to share familiar songs with family and friends. I felt a sense of peace when I played accordion because I was completely immersed in creating the sound. I felt like my body was in tune with something greater than myself.

My interest in the power of air flow was ignited through my study of the accordion, and I became fascinated with playing a wind instrument. It was the next step in the right direction. I was given a fife and a marching band uniform. It was not as easy to produce a sound as it looked. I could read music and the fingerings were simple. The challenge was producing a solid tone quality. I practiced diligently and excelled quickly. I have many happy memories of marching together in the Notre Dame Fife and Drum Corps and with my high school and college marching band. My father's favorite song echoed in my ears, "Oh, when the saints go marching in, Oh, when the saints go marching in, Oh Lord I want to be in that number, Oh, when the saints go marching in." The rhythm of our marching and the sound of our corps brought me a sense of unity and connection with others that allowed me to continue my musical development as a wind player.

Something deep down inside of me still yearned for a musical voice that would resonate with my heart and help me to express my emotions. One of my father's favorite sayings was, "Let's sit down and have a cup of coffee together and talk about it. You must never give up." I am eternally grateful to him for this lesson, as it has allowed me to slow down, share my thoughts and feelings, gather a new perspective, and make better decisions in my life. Plato once wrote, "An unexamined life is not worth living." These wise and true words seem to be lost in the push button society we are building today, and I wanted more than that. One of my mother's favorite sayings was, "You never know when a miracle may happen. It could happen today, tomorrow, or a year from now." She also taught me to never give up. As I persevered in finding my musical voice, the miracle finally happened.

Sometimes, God reveals His answers through nature,

and sometimes He reveals His answers through grace. I was blessed to receive the answer through both nature and grace. While my brother was playing his first flute solo for the high school spring concert, a bee landed on his nose and he stopped playing. He did not get stung, but he never played the flute again. As the next sibling in line, I was given a flute and a story to overcome.

Did my flute come first, or my story to overcome? As I have grown in wisdom, I realize that people are complex, and life is complicated. Somehow, today I realize it does not really matter which came first. What matters is that I take the lessons I learned in life to help others. When we encounter the essence of who we truly are and live our lives out of this center, life becomes harmonious and true joy our way of being.

As the next sibling in line at age 8, the flute was given to me, and with much diligence and practice, I found my "voice". Drawn to the sound of the instrument, I learned discipline and fortitude, and progressed with grace. Most teachers do not start flute students until they are at least 8 years old because of the physical requirements and the amount of coordination needed to play flute. There is a special "Suzuki Flute" that is made with a curved head joint so students can begin their study of flute a few years earlier with a shorter instrument to hold. Diaphragmatic breathing is essential to producing a beautiful and sustained tone quality throughout all three registers. Breath support and control come with years of long tones and detailed phrasing exercises. The proper embouchure is essential to pure tone quality development. The fingerings on the flute are quite simple as each finger is assigned to one key, and it is either pressed down or lifted up in a different pattern for each note. The most difficult note to play on the flute is a C#, mainly because it is played with only the right pinky, and the thumbs struggle to create a tri-pod to hold the flute while the musician blows across the embouchure hole. As the flute moves out of place, so does the intonation and tone quality of C#. It is interesting to note that the key to playing C# is balance, and this note's resonance is most known for its healing properties.

The right teacher can make all the difference in a student's life. I was blessed to study with the following professional flautists who formed my flute education: Kathy Curran, Allison Loddengard, Heather Kent, Peter Bloom, and Kris Krueger. Each one guided me into excellence. I performed with the Cape Ann Symphony Orchestra, the New Hampshire Philharmonic Orchestra, the Gordon College Flute Choir, and various other ensembles. I was a faculty member of the Cape Ann Conservatory, Ipswich School District, Gloucester School District, and Rockport School District in Massachusetts, and the Stratham and Dover School Districts in New Hampshire. I was also a faculty member of the Manchester Community Music School, The Derryfield School (volunteer), Portsmouth Christian Academy, all while maintaining my own private flute studio. Music opened many doors to me, and I stepped through each one with grace.

While I was raising my children, I also became a licensed Kindermusik Educator. This is an exceptional early childhood music program that offers an integrated and evidence-based program that develops the physical, mental, and emotional needs of children ages 0-7 years old. When I set my opening day of classes to be September 12, 2001, I had no idea what would happen the day before in our country. My work with integrating music with trauma informed care began in this Kindermusik program.

I had two classes of twelve students, ages 3-5 years old, scheduled for my opening day. Parents were required to stay with their children in class to share the experience with them and learn how to develop it further at home. When the students and parents arrived, they were accompanied by siblings of all ages and grandparents. As I faced the look of fear in their eyes, I humbly asked Our Lord to be with me and fill me with His grace. I smiled and said, "All are welcome. We will come together today and sing our way through this storm." Within moments of singing and dancing to the music, the fear dissipated, and the strength of our connection filled the room with hope. Yes, music has the power to elevate the soul to the realm of divine existence.

My work as a Kindermusik Educator offered me experience in leading youth choirs while developing my knowledge and experience with the healing effects of choral singing. The world changed after the terrorist attack on our country, and I searched for a way to stop fear from overtaking the lives of our children and families. God continued to guide me in the right direction, and I was asked to direct a youth choir for a world-renown musician, Peter Mayer.

The Peter Mayer Group is directed by Peter Mayer, lead guitarist for Jimmy Buffet and fellow Christian homeschooler. Peter's father was a Lutheran pastor and raised their family in India. His music was filled with love, faith, and charity to others. My heart has always searched for ways to share in the blessings of living a Christian life with others and helping those in need connect to the peace, love, and joy of knowing Jesus. For 10 years, I directed the youth choir for the Peter Mayer "Stars and Promises" Holiday Concert in New Hampshire. We performed at the University of New Hampshire Paul

Creative Arts Center, the Rochester Opera House, and the Dover High School Auditorium, and we raised money for local charities each year.

Our concert at the Rochester Opera House was one to remember. One of our favorite songs to sing with the Peter Mayer Group was "The Little Drummer Boy". R. Scott Bryan is the percussionist for the group, and he inspired all of us with his surrender to the rhythm and power of drumming. I wanted the audience to be part of the stage experience and to feel the universal beat resonating through their minds and hearts. Peter was very gracious and open to my new ideas. We had the youth choir march in through the aisles while beating "Pa Rum Pa Pum Pum" with their hands. It was a holy moment in my life as the children walked through the aisles, and we watched people of all ages join in the "beat of life". Yes, the audience started "drumming" along with the youth as they walked toward the stage. The gift we brought to Our Mighty King was the gift of unity.

The younger children and I were on stage with the Peter Mayer Group, singing and drumming together, as we awaited the arrival of the youth choir. The Rochester Opera House was a lovely old auditorium filled with carved wooden arches, stunning balconies, and secret stairways. The acoustics were excellent, and the seating was intimate. We were singing "The Little Drummer Boy", which is written in a minor key, when all of a sudden, the audience started to giggle. Trust me, this is not an experience that any performer desires.

The nervous giggle started softly and grew quickly. What were they giggling at? Did one of my children fall out of line? Did someone sing or play something out of tune? Like the tale of *The Emperor's New Clothes,* I think everyone on stage felt a bit "naked" as we continued to sing. Praise God, Marc Torlina, the string bass player seized the moment and responded to the audience's emotion with a change of tune. Without a word to the rest of the band, Marc transitioned the group into a joyful Christmas carol that matched the sound of the giggling audience. We all followed. It was as if this transition had been planned and executed in the divine realms. The music met the emotion and the emotion resolved. A few moments later, Marc transitioned us back to finish "The Little Drummer Boy" with a silent sigh of relief as we reached the newborn King.

None of us knew what the laughter had been about until after the concert, but that holy moment of experiencing the connection in between music, emotion, and seamless communication lives forever in my mind and heart. Yes, God was preparing me for a new direction in my life, and it had come in the form of a bat. A bat, you ask? Yes, a bat was awakened by the sounds of the drum, and it flew out to circle the audience while we were singing. The giggle had a touch of anxiety and a sprinkle of anticipation. What would he do? Where would he go? Was he looking for the newborn King, too? My goodness, Our Lord and our music had hit a grand slam!

As I raised my children and taught in public, private, Christian, and charter schools, I continued to witness the disintegration of our culture and the anxiety it was producing in our families. This work led me to pursue a master's degree in social work at the University of New Hampshire, focusing on the application of music as medicine.

To be honest, I was overwhelmed at the research knowledge base that was already in existence. It validated my experience working with children and families in music education for over twenty years. The field was growing rapidly, and the competition for knowledge intense. I prayed and followed the next right step while building this important resource. The Music for Healing and Transition Program at Concord Hospital offered me the science of music as medicine. Indeed, even Hippocrates prescribed the alternating sounds of flute and lyre to treat gout. MHTP, Inc. is an international educational certification program which is accredited through the National Standards Board for Therapeutic Musicians. Training consists of five weekend modules (eighteen hours each) and a forty-five hour internship. The modules include patient assessment and intervention, human behavior in the medical environment, scope of practice, musical proficiency, ethical and professional behavior in healthcare, and sound healing techniques. Therapeutic music is an art based on the science of sound. It is live acoustic music, played or sung, specifically tailored to an individual patient's immediate need while bringing music's intrinsic healing properties to the bedside. Therapeutic musicians provide a healing environment to help restore a state of well-being that is attuned and adjusted to each patient during a thirty minute session.

The concept that music has healing properties is not new to the twenty-first century. Philosophers and scholars of the Middle Ages believed that inaudible music was the force that held the universe in order. Acoustics was the transference of this inaudible force to the audible music produced by instruments or voices. Music was associated with the highest forms of study and was considered a sacred force that had the power to shape the morals and character of mankind. Music and speech share many characteristics of expression and communication. Both can be improvised and developed in the moment. Both can communicate and influence emotion. Both are learned through imitation and cultural conditioning. Music and speech are powerful tools of language that need to be used with sensitivity because of the evocative associations that may be connected to the experience. Some examples of the parallels between music and language are: inflection to imply a question is echoed with ascending phrases and feminine cadences; comparison and contrast is echoed with balanced phrasing of musical ideas through antecedents and consequents; and emotions are communicated through musical modes and major and minor scales.

The elements of music that may be used to adjust the music to the patient's condition include: melody (ascending, descending, conjunct, disjunct, and arched); range (high, middle, low); rhythm and meter (duple, triple, even, dotted, arrhythmic); tempo (adagio, andante, vivace); harmony (key, tonality, modes, major chords, minor chords, consonance, dissonance); tone and volume (decibel level near, decibel level far, instrument, resonance); texture. Most therapeutic musicians play at a low volume with a tone quality that is filled with harmonics. Leeds notes that the healing power of the tonality lies in the harmonics, which are produced by long term musical study of overtones (Leeds 2010, 169). For example, when a professional musician plays the lower register of a flute, it is filled with harmonics; the fundamental tone and overtones are all in tune with each other, and the resonance is spectacular.

The history of sound and music used as therapy, the physics of sound, the system of harmony, the body's role in perceiving sound, the sense of hearing, and the elements of music and their therapeutic effects are also examined in the MHTP, Inc. curriculum. The universal rhythm of a mother's heartbeat is noted for frequency, wave, pitch, amplitude, and loudness. Higher pitches produce shorter wavelengths of sound and could connect to brainwaves. Lower pitches produce longer wavelengths of sound and may connect to respiratory waves. Traditional western medicine is recognizing that the state of chronic stress experienced today leads to numerous life-threatening illnesses. The MHTP, Inc. curriculum teaches that relaxation response engaged by the parasympathetic nervous system through soothing music can be a strong complement to medical practice.

Indeed, even in times of pandemic when singing is banned from churches and public places, the ability to hum may provide significant benefits to health and wellness. Humming has been found to stimulate the inner ear, the vestibular system, and the tenth cranial nerve. The effects of humming include an increase in energy and stamina and improvement in clarity of mind, creativity, reading and comprehension, balance, coordination, and posture while balancing blood pressure, brain waves, mood, and hormones. Humming can even improve sleep cycles and strengthen the immune system. Indeed, the natural humming of cats, which we call "purring", keeps their bones and joints in perfect health.

Campbell notes that music masks unpleasant sounds and feelings, affects respiration, reduces muscle tension, increases endorphin levels, regulates stress-related hormones, boosts immune function, strengthens memory and learning, and generates a sense of safety and well-being (Campbell 2007, 64). The neurobiological foundations of music are being researched across the world as we speak. A relatively new field of study, psychoneuroimmunology is studying the communication between the immune system and the neuroendocrine system. They have found that imbalances in the neuro endocrine-immune circuitry are relevant to host defenses. The links between psychoneuroimmunology and neurologic and psychiatric diseases, infection, cardiovascular disease, addiction, and aging are at the front lines of current research. The influence of emotions on the immune system and ways in which complementary therapeutic techniques can mitigate the immune-mediated diseases deserves further research. It is a well-known belief that stressful emotions create a barrier to health. When our body's resources are engaged in the battle against stress, they are limited in the battle against illness and disease. Truly, the consideration of the power of music to reduce or alleviate stressful emotions and promote a healing environment of restoration and health for the body is essential.

As an oncology social work intern, I collaborated with the therapeutic arts department and medical team to create, develop, and implement "Creative Hearts for Teens", an integrated therapeutic approach to support teenagers with parents battling cancer. The group met once a week for a couple of hours for four consecutive weeks. Our primary purpose was to offer a safe space for teens to receive mental, emotional, and spiritual support while dealing with a parent's cancer diagnosis. Each session incorporated education, expression, and empowerment through the arts.

The first session, "Diagnosis and Dreams", was focused on creating a safe space to tell their family's cancer diagnosis story. A flute meditation was incorporated into this session to provide comfort and strength after sharing their story. The second session, "Education and Empowerment", was focused on learning about cancer diagnosis, treatment, and prognosis. As we faced the truth with grace and strength, we chose the theme song of our group to be "Fearless" by Taylor Swift. As we sang together, the teens created a "Footprints Mosaic" with the art interns. We spread a king size white sheet on the floor of the hospital conference room with a bucket of paint at each corner to hold it in place. The teens took off their shoes and "feet-painted" across the sheet. The results were stunning. The realization that we could walk this journey together and not be alone was the greatest gift of this therapeutic arts intervention. We did not make any false promises to the teens; we gave them information and education and showed them that they would not walk this journey alone. When the sheet dried, we all had tears in our eyes from the mystical heart that had appeared in the center of the sheet that was made up of all our footprints. The teens decided to cut the sheet into squares and frame these squares as gifts to the medical staff that were treating their parents.

The third session, "Love and Lessons", was an opportunity to look at what love really means in our lives: how sometimes loving someone is difficult, and that it is okay to be angry at someone you love. Yes, it was okay to feel angry about having to deal with cancer at this point in their lives. In order to express the dichotomy of emotions they felt, a drum was brought out to share for musical expression. Letting go of anger through drumming is a powerful therapeutic technique. And the last session, "Strengths and Songs", celebrated the connection we made with each other, the support system they developed, and the new coping skills the teens learned. We created "Strong Boxes" for which the teens wrote strengths they noticed in each other and then placed them into each other's boxes. A strength based and solution focused approach has always been at the core of my work.

As the teens joined to sing "Fearless", I accompanied

them on my flute, and we formed memories of unity that would remain forever. As we approached the end of these meetings, I gave each of the teens a recorder and taught them to play a few songs. Understanding that music could reduce anxiety and restore a healing environment in their home was very empowering to the teens. Indeed,

> Leading with passion is about courageously casting off fear, doubt, and limiting beliefs and giving people a sense of hope, optimism, and accomplishment. It is about bringing light in a world of uncertainty and inspiring others to do the same (Murphy 2011, 2).

As a hospice volunteer coordinator, I collaborated with the medical team to create, develop, and implement seven volunteer therapeutic arts programs. The most successful hospice volunteer program was the Therapeutic Music Program. Recalling the work of David as he played the harp for King Saul, I taught patients, families, and staff how to play the Reverie harp for their loved ones. The Reverie harp is a beautiful instrument that anyone can play. It is tuned to a pentatonic scale in the key of C major and is always harmonious when strummed. The peaceful sounds of the Reverie harp bring delight, relaxation, and tranquility. Witnessing the power of music to reduce anxiety, relieve depression, and alleviate pain was truly humbling.

I also watched the miraculous power of music awaken the minds of Alzheimer's patients. These experiences changed my life and set my feet on a new path. I will share with you three of the most significant stories of music as medicine in order for you to fully understand my passion and dedication to this work.

One afternoon, I brought two volunteers to learn how to use the Reverie harp with a patient with end stage Alzheimer's. He had just been admitted to a memory care facility, and his wife had gone home to pick up a few more of his belongings to make his room comfortable. This was probably one of the most difficult days in her life as they had been married over fifty years. After introducing myself and my two volunteers, I asked the patient if it was okay to strum the harp a little bit. The Reverie harp was tuned and ready to go. He was non-verbal and simply grunted. The nurse had given us permission to share the music with him, so I began very slowly. I played the five notes in order and watched to see if there was a note that the patient connected with. Suddenly, he took a deep breath when I played the middle pitch. I knew to stay there and strum the note rhythmically. We connected. I then began a pattern of playing back and forth between two notes, again very slowly. After a little over five minutes of introducing music to the environment, the patient responded. He lifted his hand and started strumming the same pattern I had been playing. Slowly, back and forth, and in order. I smiled. The volunteers watched in awe.

When the moment was right, I asked the patient his name. He began to speak and his words were clear and concise. His name was John. He liked the music. He loved to dance with his wife. They loved to sail together. As we took turns strumming the harp, John told me several stories about sailing with his wife, Sarah. He shared several details including dates, locations, and important memories. He had come back to life with music. Our time together lasted over an hour, and when it was time to go, I was surrounded by an audience of clinicians that were stunned.

As we were leaving the building, the director introduced me to John's wife, Sarah, who had returned from picking up more supplies from home. When I told her about our music intervention and John's response, she started sobbing with pure joy! John had remembered their sailing adventures and their life together. He was not at all lost to her. The staff in his "new home" could learn about their love for each other and their history and would take even better care of him. Indeed, on our next visit I would teach her how to use the Reverie harp with her husband and share their own special time together.

My next volunteer adventure was a sing-along at a local nursing home. I had a choir of fifteen hospice volunteers and one hundred fifty patients. We began together in the activities room with many scornful faces. Singing? What was there to sing about? As I gazed about the room and got a sense of the average age of patients and calculated what decade they had experienced when they were in their 20's, I chose appropriate music for us to sing together. Research indicates that most people best remember the music that was playing when they were 18-25 years old. Within moments, everyone was joining in the fun, and a few started asking for solos! The energy changed from silent scorn to complete glee! Residents were smiling and connecting with each other, and staff members began to sing along, too! Volunteers had fun taking turns leading their favorite songs, and some even added a few movements to the music. The time went by very quickly as we were united in song, and joy radiated around the room! My volunteers and I could not wait to go to the next health care facility!

"Grace" was in her early 60's and was diagnosed with early onset dementia. She was in a locked facility. When we entered her room, she was incoherent and her words were scrambled. I experienced a moment of doubt that we would be able to connect with her. I had a team of three volunteers with me, and after introducing ourselves, we began to sing a few of the favorites from her college years. Within minutes we witnessed the miracle of music restore order to the mind. Grace's thoughts cleared, and she joined in the singing, knowing the words better than we did! We sang with her for about a half hour and had a lovely conversation with her before leaving the room. It was as if the sunlight of the spirit had entered her soul. We were completely speechless on the way home.

For the past 7 years, I have contributed to the field of music as medicine with developing therapeutic arts programs in oncology, hospice, homecare, and memory care. I have developed a course on Music as Medicine and presented it at Granite State College OLLI Program, the Thompson Center on Lourdes, and Ridgeview Highlands. I have presented my work to the Social Work Oncology Group of New Hampshire, the Chamber of Commerce of Concord, New Hampshire, The Merrimack County Resource Group at Riverbend Counseling, and the Stroke Support Group at HealthSouth Hospital.

With the hope to better serve the growing needs of our world in crisis, I conducted a sabbatical to assess, research, and develop this valuable resource. I strongly adhere to the social work code of ethics and the moral beliefs of Catholicism.

During this research sabbatical, I came to personally understand that the frequency of pitch and the rhythm of sound can be employed to affect brain waves, respiratory waves, and heart rates. When I realized our vital signs were like a set of gears, each influencing the other, I fell to my knees with a vision of the power of sound to help or hurt human beings. I placed my work on the altar of Christ and asked for His direction. My work transitioned from a clinical perspective to a Catholic perspective.

Truly, God loves music. I can hear his angels singing, "Holy, Holy, Holy is the Lord God Almighty, Heaven and Earth are full of Your Glory! Hosanna in the Highest!" Revelation 4:8 tells us that the angels sing, "day and night they never cease to sing..." Why did God give us this powerful gift of music? What did he want us to do with it?

It took me years to understand the gifts of anointed music, and each time I experienced it, I was drawn into the heart of Christ and enveloped in His love. Saint Augustine said that "He who sings prays twice." Anointed music has a great power to open our hearts to the love of God. When a heart that truly loves God sings to Him with praise and thanksgiving, their music is anointed. Psalm 22:3 reminds us that God is "enthroned on the praises of Israel." God loves praise music! When we bring Him our hearts filled with gratitude for His glory connected to voices speaking the Word of the Lord, we open a door to heaven that allows His love to flow into and through us. When we sing God's praises, God's love pours into us, and miracles, healings, and conversions happen. I know because I, myself, have experienced this healing through music. In September 2019, I attended Father Greg Bramlage's parish mission at Saint Pius X Parish in Appleton, Wisconsin and received a profound healing of my vision through praise and worship music.

The science of music as medicine led me to the source of all love and goodness, and the splendor and glory of Our Almighty and Powerful God. The culmination of these efforts has resulted in this book, *Canto Divina.*

18 Canto Divina

A Brief History of Music as Medicine

Everyone loves the biblical story of David and Goliath. A small, innocent shepherd boy killing a monstrous pagan warrior with just a rock and a sling is the epitome of good overcoming evil. However, this was just the beginning of David's life. After David became a military hero, he became a medical hero. King Saul summoned David to his kingdom to learn more about this shepherd boy who had such courage. As they developed a strong bond, which included the love of Saul's son Jonathan, Saul began to trust David with his innermost struggles. Indeed, Saul suffered from depression. He had seen the face of God, and nothing else would please him. David became a favorite of King Saul after he played his harp to help relieve the king's depression. David composed and performed over seventy psalms for King Saul that are recorded in the Bible.

The psalms are sacred songs that were accompanied by stringed instruments and were written to help express emotions and open the pathway to communion with God. They are still a regular part of the Catholic Mass, which is said every day, in every Catholic Church, all around the world. Although there is not an accurate census of the number of Catholic churches in the world, there are over 250,000 parishes which include several churches, and Mass is said in each one between seven and twenty times per week. Certainly, one could closely estimate that over 1 billion psalms are sung with instrumental accompaniment each year for 1.2 billion Catholics all over the world. In truth, the psalms unify our faith and our church through word and through music.

David was a true hero. He saved Israel from the Philistines; he healed King Saul's depression; he forgave Saul for turning on him and pursuing him all over the country for seven years; he conquered Jerusalem and returned the Ark of the Covenant to the city. David is also a human being. After all his successes, he falls in love with another man's wife, Bathsheba, and has her husband, Uriah the Hittite, killed in battle. Although David returns to God for forgiveness and receives it immediately, there are consequences of his sins— both good and bad. His son Absalom is killed in battle, and his son Solomon becomes his successor. King Solomon builds the temple of the Ark of the Covenant and leads the way for the Messiah. The Old Testament book, entitled the "Song of Songs", is attributed to Solomon—it is also known as the "Song of Solomon". This is a beautiful family story of power, love, forgiveness, and the music that connects them all.

During the Ancient Greek Period from 700-480 BC, there were many advances in poetry, art, and technology. It was a very sophisticated time that led to the development of the city-state, the polis. This political formation is the foundation of democracy. During this time, the Greeks created and worshiped their own beautiful, radiant gods. Most of the Greek gods were tall and handsome, but far from perfect. The gods lived on top of Olympus, a very high mountain in Greece that seemed to the people of that time to touch the sky. The Greeks worshiped the gods, and the gods honored Mother Earth, who the Greeks believed was the beginning of all life.

They also believed that Zeus was the lord of the universe. Zeus was known to be stronger than all the other gods together. Zeus and his wife Leto had twins named Apollo and Artemis. Artemis became goddess of the hunt, and Apollo became the god of prophecy, music, and knowledge. It is interesting that the gifts of prophecy, music, poetry, and knowledge were linked together in the god who was to become the father of the god of medicine.

Apollo is often depicted playing a golden lyre and is also known as the god of healing. Apollo is noted for giving the science of medicine to the Greeks as well as the wisdom of truth and light. The Greeks believed that to have health and healing there must be a harmonious ordering of all the vital forces within an organism. Just like all the strings of a lyre must be in tune with each other, all of the rhythmic systems of an organism must also resonate together. Indeed, the brain, the heart, and the lungs are all intricately connected by rhythm. Fittingly, Apollo's son, Asclepius, became the god of medicine, and Apollo is the first god mentioned in the Hippocratic Oath.

Hippocrates was born c. 460 BC on the island of Cos, Greece. He was an Ancient Greek physician and is regarded as the "Father of Medicine". He is revered as the ideal physician due to his ethical standards in medical practice. The Hippocratic Oath focuses on the integrity of the profession, benevolence, and respect for human dignity in the practice of medicine. Hippocrates understood the need for evidence-based knowledge that provided a holistic approach for each patient. He highlighted the need for harmony between the individual and his social and natural environment. As wars were a common occurrence in ancient Greece, Hippocrates faced the need for interventions in trauma care. His prescriptions included the use of drug therapy, diets, physical and mental exercises, as well as divine solicitation.

Hippocrates believed that the role of music and theater was essential in the treatment of physical and mental illnesses and the improvement of human behavior. Indeed, Hippocrates seemed to understand the importance of processing emotions to increase health and wellness. As music is one of the languages of emotion, it can help a patient release emotional blocks and open the channels of blood flow to heal the body more fully. In fact, Hippocrates prescribed specific music to heal certain diseases. His use of the flute and harp as alternating melodies to treat gout is fascinating. He also noted that those who had listened to sacred religious melodies, which addressed the needs of the soul, resembled other patients that had undergone medical treatment, mental renewal, and restoration. Theater, especially ancient tragedies, added the visual component to music with a stunning and illuminating conclusion. Hippocrates noted, it was a system of interventions that had the most positive outcome on health and wellness (Kleisiaris 2014).

The Middle Ages (450-1500 AD) were a cultural period of great darkness. This time period included the Hundred Year's War, the Crusades, plagues, religious persecution, and minimal education. It was a time that required a system of health and wellness to overcome the dismal quality of life. Indeed, Pope Saint Gregory the Great is well known for collecting and codifying a system of chants that accompanied the liturgy of the Roman Catholic Church and the Divine Office. Gregorian chant was initially unaccompanied sung prayer in Latin which evolved into accompanied unison singing of psalms, biblical verses, and hymns. Some of these include the parts of the Mass, such as the Gloria, Sanctus, Kyrie, Agnus Dei, and Alleluia. A similar type of sung prayer is thought to have originated in the synagogues at the time of Jesus. It has been a central expression of natural beauty and musical excellence for many centuries.

Gregorian chant is composed on a system of modes that are structured to reflect an open, spacious, and prayerful like feeling which open the doors to heaven for the listener. The modes are named after geographic regions of Greece in order to honor the Greek musicians that created them. They include the Lydian, Ionian, Mixolydian, Dorian, Aeolian, and Phrygian modes which are ephemeral in quality and elude gravity. The movement from one mode to the other is relatively simple, and one can easily compose a cathartic chant that releases pent up emotions and unblocks the blood flow needed to heal the body and soul.

Pope Saint Gregory believed that music was the inaudible force that held the universe in order while connecting the body and soul. In his eyes, audible music was an acoustic manifestation of these forces and therefore required the highest form of study. Gregorian chant was known to be a sacred force which held the power to shape human behavior. Indeed, Charlemagne, King of the Franks (768—814 AD) ordered Gregorian chant to be sung in his kingdom. Eventually Gregorian chant merged with the more common Gallican chant and became the assimilated version that has come down to us through the ages.

According to the Stanford Encyclopedia of Philosophy, the most important medieval musical treatise in Islamic lands, which also includes philosophical sections, was written by Al

Farabi. His Great Book of Music is considered a work of art. Scholars have disputed his native origin, but most conclude that he lived from 870 AD to 950 AD and spent time in Iraq, Syria, and Damascus. He was instrumental in transmitting the doctrines of Plato and Aristotle in the Muslim world.

Al Farabi is known to some as the second greatest philosopher after Aristotle. Al Farabi combined the study of philosophy with that of logic, ethics, metaphysics, mathematics, and music. He noted that to be a great teacher one must be of good character, free from cravings—addiction, a physical craving that takes over the soul-- and seek only the truth. He considered the beginning of any lesson to be ethics, because it embraces the love of good and the hatred of evil. He also believed that music addressed the soul of the listener and aided them to rise above their circumstances and discern right from wrong.

After ethics, according to Al Farabi, the next important development of an education is mathematics. In the study of mathematics, he included: arithmetic, geometry, the science of perspectives, astronomy, music, dynamics, and the science of machines. It is very interesting to note that Al Farabi did not include the study of medicine within the sciences. Farabi inculcated his study of music with a long application of listening followed by a practical application of science. He created instruments that are tuned in a specific way to restore order to scales and music theory. Al Farabi understood the essential nature of intonation in music practice. As the frequency of each pitch must be matched by any group of musicians wishing to perform together, his perception of the nature of this element in music study indicates his reputation as a great thinker. Al Farabi also approved of the discipline needed to pursue the study of music. He understood that only by obedience to rules and regulations are we set free to create and explore the beauty of life.

Saint Hildegard von Bingen, (1098—1179) is most known for her unique and glorious music that she composed as prioress of a Benedictine monastery in Rupertsberg, Germany. Hildegard von Bingen was born of noble parents and began having mystical visions at three years old. Her first book, Scivias, was written over a period of ten years and details all her visions. Her informal music training was based upon the Roman Mass chants and simple choir instruction from her former prioress, Blessed Jutta. She composed seventy-seven lyric poems with musical settings, wrote two treatises on medicine and natural history, several books, and almost four hundred letters. Several miracles are associated with Saint Hildegard von Bingen, who was canonized by Pope Benedict XVI in 2012.

Saint Hildegard von Bingen wrote *Physica*, a book on health and healing, and she also wrote On Natural Philosophy of Medicine: Cures and Cause. This praiseworthy medieval doctor of the church was a pharmacist, theologian, philosopher, poet, and polymath. It is interesting to note that she preached during a time when the church was criticized for many abuses. Her work was rediscovered in the 1980's when the church was again under scrutiny for sins of the flesh. Indeed, her music has recently become somewhat popular on social media and may be helping to restore the dignity of living a virtuous life.

The Renaissance period was a welcome refuge for European culture. As scholars returned to the study of the Ancient Greek and Roman philosophers, moral and ethical values were reignited, and the study of modern science began. With the invention of the printing press by Johannes Gutenberg, sheet music could be printed, and musical groups could perform together with ease. New instruments were invented, including the harpsichord and the violin. Many influential families, including the famous Medicis, moved to Florence, Italy to rebuild their lives. Most of them supported the development of various artistic endeavors. The Catholic Church was a prominent force in establishing this rebirth of the arts. The visual arts took precedence with Leonardo da Vinci painting *The Last Supper* and the *Mona Lisa*, Michelangelo painting the ceiling of the Sistine Chapel and sculpting both *David* and the *Pieta*, and Donatello creating the statue of *Saint Mark* in Florence, Italy. The development of sacred music also prospered due to the benefactors of the Catholic Church.

Italian composer, Palestrina, is well-known for his motets and Masses for the Church. He composed *Missa Papae Marcelli* for Pope Julius III. He was a prolific composer and completed one hundred four Masses, sixty-eight offertories, over three hundred motets, at least seventy-two hymns, thirty-five Magnificats, eleven litanies, four lamentations, one hundred forty madrigals, and nine organ ricercari (Bach Cantatas Website). He suffered many losses in his life, including the death of his wife, two sons, and a brother to the plague outbreaks in the 1570's. His music is renowned for its spiritual qualities and technical mastery. He may have found solace in composing and performing these masterpieces and lived what is considered a long life in Renaissance time, 60 years.

The secular madrigals that Palestrina composed were originally for two to eight voices, unaccompanied. However, in modern times they can be played by instrumentalists and are quite dance-like. It seems that his hope was to uplift the spirits of those around him with music that was light, playful, and rhythmic. A typical two stanza madrigal reflects the form of the poetry that was written during this same time period. The form of a madrigal was typically AAB, with both stanzas A being sung to the same music and stanza B completing the thought with concluding sound. This was how the poetry of this time connected to the healing rhythm of music.

William Shakespeare, English poet and playwright, lived during the Elizabethan age of the Renaissance period. In this dynamic time, Shakespeare helped to voice the concerns of the general populace that were facing significant scientific and geographic discoveries. Shakespeare's plays were well received as they were an effective method of processing the emotions of these times of change. With plagues, wars, and famine occurring at the same time as explorations of the "New World", a place to pause and "be still" was needed. Shakespeare's plays were performed in the Globe Theatre in London which was close to the Thames River. Couples could enjoy an evening out, let go of any tension through the creative genius of Shakespeare's plays, and walk along the river deciding to just go with the flow. Little did they know that much of the voicing of Shakespeare's poetry and plays were written in iambic pentameter, which happens to correspond to the rhythm of a healthy heartbeat. The sound of Shakespeare's plays actually helped to stabilize the heartbeat and reduce the anxiety of the audience. Many would be surprised to learn that Shakespeare was also a Catholic.

The lute was the primary instrument of composition and performance during the Renaissance. As in the time of David, stringed instruments brought the most healing to listeners. The lute was pear shaped, with six strings, and made of wood. Shakespeare noted that the lute had an innate ability to transform listeners to a state of ecstasy. He wrote, "Now divine aire, now is his soule ravisht, is it not strange that sheepes guts should hale soules out of mens bodies?" (William Shakespeare, *Much Ado About Nothing*, Act II, Scene 3).

The music of the Baroque Period offered a time of order to help stabilize the new world. The beauty and simplicity of Bach's *Saint Matthew's Passion*, the *Brandenburg Concertos*, the *Goldberg Variations*, the *Cello Suites*, the *Violin Sonatas*, and the *Well-Tempered Clavier* are world renown. The innate order of music composition in Bach's works brings lasting peace to all his listeners.

The music of the Classical Period brought the gifts of Amadeus Mozart to the stage. He was a child prodigy devoted to composition and performance who wrote in all musical genres with success. Mozart's command of form, his musical taste, and his range of expression have memorialized him as a universal composer and performer. Indeed, the profound effects of his music on universal listeners can be found in the "bible" of music healing entitled, *The Mozart Effect*, by Don Campbell.

Johannes Brahms was a German composer, pianist, and conductor of the Romantic Period. He was born in Hamburg to a Lutheran family. His greatest works include the *Piano Concerto No. 1*, the *Violin Concerto, Symphony No. 1*, and *Symphony No. 4*. Of course, the beauty and elegance of his music has helped many children fall asleep peacefully across the world.

In the Modern Era of music, we find a time of great change and discourse. A leading composer from Julliard

School of Music, Dr. Samuel Zyman, connects the world of music and medicine, as he is also an M.D. from the National Autonomous University of Mexico. He received a Mozart Medal in 1998, and his compositions have been performed in the United States, Mexico, Canada, Europe, and South America. As the world discerns new opportunities and grows in many directions, the music of this time reflects the exploration of sound and new ideas.

The Post Modern Era of music brings the world to a new time of skepticism, relativism, and suspicion in a world of political and economic power struggles. Composers noted for their importance in this era include: John Adams, Thomas Ades, Robert Ashey, Luciano Berio, Harrison Birtwistle, Pierre Boulez, John Cage, and Phillip Glass. As the disorder of music and society grows, it is interesting to note that order has begun to return through the rediscovery of Gregorian chant. How exciting to learn of the Neumz project which includes the entire Gregorian chant repertory, recorded by the community of Benedictine nuns of the Abbey of Notre-Dame de Fidélité at Jouques, in the Ecclesiastical province of Marseille, France.

In this historical time period of pandemics, violence, and disorder, I offer this work of *Canto Divina* in an effort to restore the order and life of Jesus Christ here on earth.

Deo Gratias.

Singing for Health and Wellness

My approach to health and wellness has always included the integration of physical, mental, emotional, social, and spiritual vitality. Perhaps this is the primary reason I have been drawn to the health and wellness benefits of singing. Physically, one stands and breathes deeply while singing which exercises the respiratory system. Mentally, one reads notes, rhythms, and words simultaneously to stimulate the mind. Emotionally, music connects to the heart and powerfully expresses our feelings. Socially, singing in a choir or performing with an orchestra are truly the most unifying experiences of belonging to a higher purpose. Spiritually, when singing Christian music, with a heart open to God, His healing love pours into and through us. With so many demands placed on our life in this new technology era, the most effective use of time spent on health and wellness is singing.

The power of music to draw out strong emotional responses and affect body chemistry has been studied by artists, scientists, and philosophers since the Ancient Greeks in the classical times of Plato and the Academy of Athens. Research on the effects of choral singing and music listening on the immune system and stress are garnering more attention in behavioral medicine (Kreutz et al. 2004, 624). Indeed, over the last two decades there has been a significant increase of interest in the potential contribution of the arts in relation to medicine, healthcare, and health promotion (Clift and Hancox 2001, 248). The Health Education Authority of the United Kingdom noted:

> The arts clearly have a potential to make a major contribution to our health, well-being and life skills. It is important, however, to capture the evidence of the impact of the arts on health to ensure proper recognition of their effect and the availability of appropriate levels of investment to sustain any positive influences (Clift and Hancox 2001, 248).

As singing is probably the most common everyday musical activity present in all cultures, is open to everyone, and requires minimal financial investment to participate, the possibility of finding a positive connection between singing and health and wellness is of immense value to our society. The ability to sing together in "virtual choirs" in a world of pandemics exponentially grows the importance of this research.

A review of the literature suggests the following indications of the power of singing to provide health and wellness benefits:

Choral Singing and Immune System Changes

In a pioneering study, Beck, Cesario, Yousefi, and Enamoto examined the endocrine effects of singing in choristers. Elevated levels of Secretory Immunoglobulin A (SIgA), an antibody that plays a critical role in mucosal immunity, have been linked to positive emotional arousal, relaxation, positive mood, and pleasurable social events (Beck et al. 1999, 88). A professional performing group of one hundred eighty singers with a mean age of 46.4 years were randomly selected to produce a relatively equal proportion of male and female participants. An early choral rehearsal that lasted 2 ½ hours and a late choral rehearsal that lasted 1 ½ hours were held one week apart. The choir members gathered to sing Beethoven's Missa Solemnis. Saliva samples were taken before and after both rehearsals and performance. The results displayed strong increases in SIgA after singing in an early or late choir rehearsal, or during a choir performance.

In a further study, Kreutz, Bongard, Rohrmann, Hodapp, and Grebe compared subjective and physiological responses produced by choral singing with those from listening to music and actively singing. Given the previous research done, it was expected that singing choral music would raise SIgA levels and provide a positive emotional effect in both experiences. An amateur choir that included twenty-three female singers and eight male singers, with an age range of 29-74 years old, was used for this study. Choral singing was experienced as a 1 hour session of singing Mozart's Requiem. Saliva testing was performed at the beginning and end of each session using a Sarstedt Salivette. One week later, the group experienced the second 1 hour session of listening to Mozart's Requiem, which was held in the same location. It also included before and after saliva testing (Kreutz et al. 2004, 627). The results indicated that SIgA increased significantly with singing and stayed the same with listening. This confirms the previous study by Beck et. al (1999) acknowledging that choral singing has a positive effect on SIgA levels.

Choral Singing and Stress Reduction

Medical research has shown that increased cortisol levels are directly related to stressful life experiences. Although pleasant emotional states are associated with decreased cortisol levels, it has not been found that relaxation reduced cortisol levels in saliva. It is also noted that the effects of positive psychological states from participation in a professional chorus on SIgA and cortisol levels are mediated by amount of practice, levels of cognition, and social support (Beck et al. 1999, 89). The relationship between singing and stress levels after performance was also found to be modified by a singer's perception of the performance outcome (Beck et al. 1999, 103). This indicates that regardless of rehearsal time or performance focus, choral singing has a positive impact on SIgA levels even though performances are naturally associated with higher degrees of anxiety. It seems that in a chorus, the large group naturally shares the stress of delivering a high-level performance due to the nature of choral singing. As a choral singer, one must humbly surrender their individual breathing, pulse, and tonality to the greater good and unity of sound of the choral group. A choir is only as good as its weakest singer. The social emotional impact of working together to form the best possible outcome for the group is clearly beneficial to all members.

Choral Singing and COPD

Bonilha, Onofre, Vieira, Prado, and Martinez examined the

effects of weekly singing classes on maximal respiratory pressures, spirometry measures, and quality of life levels of forty-three patients with chronic obstructive pulmonary disease in Brazil. Patients who were invited to participate in the study had a diagnosis of COPD, were former smokers, and had been in stable clinical condition for at least two months (Bonilha et al. 2009, 2). The patients were randomly chosen for a singing group which participated in twenty-four weeks of singing classes that met once a week for one hour, and a control group, which attended the same number of weekly classes but were given artwork by a physiotherapist. Medical measurements of respiratory pressures and spirometry data were taken after completion of the twenty-four week session.

Since respiration plays a key role in singing, and the practice of singing involves strong and fast inspirations followed by long, regulated expirations, it was demonstrated that choral singing helps to develop better breathing coordination and reduces the stress of challenging respiratory emotions. This study indicated that singing is not only a feasible treatment for patients with COPD, but that choral singing lessons were shown to provide a pleasant way of training expiratory muscles, improvement of endurance, strength, and exercise performance while also enhancing the quality of life for COPD patients (Bonilha et al. 2009, 6).

Choral Singing and Psychological Health and Wellness

Clift and Hancox conducted two exploratory studies of the perceived benefits of choral singing with a university college choral society. In the first study, eighty-four members completed a brief, open-ended questionnaire about their experiences during rehearsals and the benefits they received. The majority of respondents reported that they benefited socially (87%), emotionally (75%), physically (75%), and spiritually (49%) (Clift and Hancox 2001, 251). A content analysis also identified common health benefit themes: improved lung function and breathing, improved mood, and stress reduction.

In the second study, ninety-one members of the college choral ensemble filled out a structured questionnaire which consisted of thirty-two positively worded statements about the impact of choral singing on psycho-physiological health. A principal components analysis found the scope of benefits associated with singing include: well-being and relaxation, breathing and posture, social, spiritual, emotional, and heart and immune system functioning (Clift and Hancox 2001, 253). The results of this second study indicated that at least 93% of respondents agreed that singing makes their mood more positive, 71% felt it improves their mental well-being, 79% felt it helps to reduce stress, and 80% agreed that singing helps them to relax (Clift and Hancox 2001, 253).

In an additional study of how participation in choirs impacts the health and wellness of not only college students and adults, but children as well, Chorus America tracked the trends in chorus participation from their 2003 baseline study and illuminated the role of choral participation in childhood education and development. The mission of Chorus America is to build a transparent choral community database so that more people become aware of the positive effects of choral singing in the United States of America (Chorus America 2009). As was noted in their Chorus Impact Study in 2009, choral singing continues to be the most popular form of participation in the performing arts, and children who sing in choruses have increased academic success and learn valuable life skills. This affirms the previous results by Clift and Hancox that choristers reported being happier with their lives and enjoying positive social relationships. I believe these results increase the need to better understand the linking mechanism between choral singing and health and wellness.

Most importantly, the Chorus Impact Study is the first of its kind to explore the value of singing for children as viewed by parents and educators. The online survey conducted of five hundred parents and three hundred educators (K-12) indicated that socio-economic status and race were not statistically significant factors in choral participation responses. It is also interesting to note that the diversity of educators from all disciplines almost unanimously agreed about the positive impact choruses have on children and their environment. It was reported by 61% of parents and 88% of educators that after joining a choir a child's academic performance is improved. 71 % of parents and 94% of educators also agree that a child's self-confidence is positively impacted by participation in a chorus. Similar to what was reported in previous studies, participants in choruses also demonstrate improved memory skills, better cognitive abilities, and overall improved physical condition. Educators most emphatically report that chorus participation makes students better members in other groups (93%), and a chorus also adds to a school's overall sense of community and school spirit (91%). To better promote health and wellness to children in school choirs, I believe this study can be very useful in promoting health and wellness benefits through the arts and supporting the continued development of school choirs (Chorus America 2009).

In a large cross-national survey conducted by Clift and Hancox a significant degree of internal validity emerged from a sample of 1124 choral singers who completed the World Health Organization questionnaire of health and well-being. Although women were more likely to report positive benefits of choral singing than men, a majority of respondents scored well above the scale midpoint of "good" to "excellent" self-assessed psychological well-being. Most importantly, it was found that the respondents in the lowest third of the psychological well-being scale demonstrated the highest third on the effects of singing scale. These respondents reported enduring mental health problems, significant family problems, physical health difficulties and bereavement concerns. This most recent study identified the mechanisms of improved health and well-being from singing as positive effects, focused concentration, controlled deep breathing, social support, cognitive stimulation, and regular commitment (Clift et al. 2010, 90).

Singing and Health: A Systematic Summary

Clift, Hancox, Staricoff, and Whitmore systematically identified, grouped, evaluated, and synthesized the existing English-language research involving choral singing and health in a thirty-five paper meta-analysis (Clift et al. 2008, 5). Studies were then grouped by the following characteristics: qualitative, questionnaires, quantitative, objective measures of physiological health, mental and physical health, physical performance, and large-scale epidemiological research. The recurrent themes of the effects of group singing were identified as follows: physical relaxation, emotional release, positive mood, greater emotional and physical well-being, increased energy, stimulation of cognitive capacities (attention, concentration, memory, learning), collective bonding, supportive social environment, sense of contribution, personal transcendence, self-confidence, self-esteem, therapeutic for long standing psychosocial issues, exercise of the lungs, discipline of the skeletal-muscular system, and a sense of purpose and motivation for being (Clift et al. 2008, 6). This comparative study of the literature significantly validated the positive impact of choral singing on health and wellness.

The Moral Power of Music

Moral formation is the formation of the will and the emotions, accustoming them to delight in their proper objects. The connection between music and the formation of virtue becomes clear when we realize that the virtues of fortitude and temperance are concerned with ordering our emotions according to logic. These virtues perfect our emotions so that we seek what is good and not what is evil. Music moves man to take delight in the emotions that the music creates. The repeated listening of virtuous music develops a quality of mind that becomes accustomed to feeling right emotions. With this connection between music and emotion, the formation of good character can be developed through active listening to the appropriate modes, tempos, and melodies of pure music.

Music can imitate a reasonable, ordered, honorable, virtuous emotion; in which case music helps dispose man to the virtuous and honorable ordering of his life. Indeed, Plato noted in his Republic, "Musical training is a more potent instrument that any other, because rhythm and harmony find their way into the inward places of the soul." Thoreau indicated that music can destroy a civilization. Truly, the power of music to secure or destroy the moral formation of a man, and therefore, a civilization, is essential to consider in the search for better health and wellness today. As Mike Aquilina notes in his book, *How the Choir Converted the World: Through Hymns, With Hymns, and In Hymns,* even St. Augustine's conversion happened through the sound of music.

Canto Divina

The Lord asks us to pray without ceasing. Jesus prays when His mission is revealed by the Father, before He calls the Apostles, when He blesses God at the multiplication of the loaves, when He transfigures on Mount Tabor, when He heals the blind, when He raises Lazarus from the dead, when He teaches the disciples how to pray, and when He blesses the little children. He begins His day early in the morning with prayer and thanksgiving which flows throughout His day. It is understood that He prayed into the fourth watch at night, keeping His eyes on His Father. Jesus taught us to pray the "Our Father" sincerely from our hearts, with humility, vigilance, perseverance, and confidence in Our Father's goodness. Our prayers link us with Jesus Christ and create a common bond of love amongst the whole human race.

The unity of the Church lives through the power of the Holy Spirit. The Holy Spirit is the "Breath of Life" for all who are baptized in Jesus Christ. The Holy Spirit is filled with the love of the Father for His Son. This Love desires to fill our hearts and heal our bodies, minds, and souls.

We receive the love of God through the sacraments of the Church: baptism, reconciliation, Holy Communion, confirmation, marriage, holy orders, and anointing of the sick. We also receive the love of God through the Liturgy of the Hours. We are united by praying the Gospels, psalms, and canticles throughout the day. We have been truly blessed with the baptism of the Holy Spirit.

Indeed, on February 18th, 1967 a group of Duquesne University students and professors experienced the boundless love of God in an outpouring of the Holy Spirit at the Ark and the Dove Retreat Center in Pittsburgh, Pennsylvania. About twenty-five members of the Duquesne University Chi Rho Scripture Study group and two professors held a retreat at The Ark and The Dove. The theme of their retreat was "The Holy Spirit." In preparation for the retreat, they were told to pray expectantly, to read "The Cross and the Switchblade," and to read the first four chapters of the Acts of the Apostles. As they gathered for each session, their professors told them to sing as a prayer the ancient hymn, "Veni Creator Spiritus" ("Come Creator Spirit"). God answered that invocation with the grace of baptism in the Holy Spirit. The outpouring of the Holy Spirit in the chapel that weekend led to the ecclesial movement known as the Catholic Charismatic Renewal (Mansfield 1992).

The love of God is now being poured out across the world in healing and deliverance missions, similar to the one started in Pittsburgh, that are focused on the love and forgiveness of Jesus Christ. The Holy Spirit is coming alive in songs of thanksgiving and praise to Our Lord. Spiritual healing, deliverance healing, inner healing, and physical healing are leading the way back to the heart of Christ. The New Evangelization in Catholicism is boundless in its desire to restore our world to the love of God.

I have created *Canto Divina* to unite our prayers and thanksgivings with the healing love of Jesus Christ, as experienced in the "Breath of Life", the Holy Spirit. As we sing, we pray twice. As we sing, we unite our minds, hearts, and bodies with the all-powerful love of God. Music opens the door to the love of God, and we receive His love.

I have modeled the structure of *Canto Divina* after the inspiring practice of *Lectio Divina*. Pope Benedict notes in his address to commemorate the 40th anniversary of the Dogmatic Constitution of Divine Revelation Dei Verbum that

> *Lectio Divina,* is the diligent reading of Sacred Scripture accompanied by prayer that brings about that intimate dialogue in which the person reading hears God who is speaking, and in praying, responds to him with trusting openness of heart.

Pope Benedict believes that *Lectio Divina* will bring a new spiritual springtime to the Church. It is my hope that the addition of singing the psalms for personal transformation in Christ will also help to bring a new spiritual springtime to our Church.

I have chosen the psalms for *Canto Divina* as they were composed under divine inspiration from the beginnings of the Church, many of them by David who had a true heart for God. David also accompanied these psalms with music that healed King Saul of several afflictions. As music is a language of emotion and the psalms are the poetry of emotion, I believe the power of uniting them in prayer may be quite significant. As we open our minds, hearts, and souls to the love of God, He will answer us abundantly with His love, forgiveness, and healing. We will be transformed.

To begin *Canto Divina* we offer the following prayer of invitation to the Holy Spirit. This prayer is most powerful when sung in Latin. It is known as the "Golden Sequence" which dates back to the thirteenth century and possibly earlier. It is attributed to Archbishop of Canterbury, Cardinal Stephen Langton. Renowned medieval theologian, Clichtoveus, in his work "Elucidatorium," notes that *Veni Sancte Spiritus* is deserving: above all praise because of its wondrous sweetness, clarity of style, pleasant brevity combined with wealth of thought (so that every line is a sentence), and finally the constructive grace and elegance displayed in the skillful and apt juxtaposition of contrasting thoughts (New Henry 1912).

Veni Sancte Spiritus

Veni, Sancte Spiritus,
Et emitte caelitus
Lucis tuae radium
Veni, pater pauperum.
Veni dator munerum,
Veni, lumen cordium.
Consolator optime,
Dulcis hospes animae
Dulce refrigerium.
In labore requies,
In aestu temperies,
In fletu solatium.
O lux beatissima,
Reple cordis intima
Tuorum fidelium.
Sine tuo numine,
Nihil est in homine,
Nihil est innoxium,
Lava quod est sordidum,
Riga quod est aridum,
Sana quod est saucium.
Flecte quod est rigidum,
Fove quod est frigidum
Rege quod est devium.
Da tuis fidelibus,
In te confidentibus,
Sacrum septenarium,
Da virtutis meritum,
Da salutis exitum,
Da perenne gaudium.
Amen. Alleluia.

Come Holy Spirit

Holy spirit! Lord of light!
From thy clear celestial height,
Thy pure, beaming radiance give:
Come, Thou, Father of the poor!
Come, with treasures which endure!
Come, Thou light of all that live!
Thou of all consolers best,
Visiting the troubled breast,
Dost refreshing peace bestow:
Thou in toil art comfort sweet;
Pleasant coolness in the heat;
Solace in the midst of woe.
Light immortal! Light divine!
Visit Thou these hearts of Thine,
And our inmost being fill.
If Thou take thy grace away,
Nothing pure in man will stay;
All his good is turn'd to ill.
Heal our wounds—our strength renew;
On our dryness pour Thy dew;
Wash the stains of guilt away:
Bend the stubborn heart and will;
Melt the frozen, warm the chill;
Guide the steps that go astray.
Thou, on those who evermore
he confess and Thee adore,
In Thy sevenfold gifts descend.
Give them comfort when they die;
Give them life with Thee on high;
Give them joys which never end.
Amen. Alleluia.
(English translation taken from catholic-link.org)

Canto means "I sing" in Latin, the universal language of the church. When we choose a psalm for transformation, we begin with listening to a musical version of the psalm to prepare our minds for the reading of the psalm. It is important to search out authentic versions of recorded psalms, preferably performed by religious orders. As we listen to the psalm being sung, we slow down our thoughts and become connected to our hearts. We are present in this holy moment.

Next, we take time to read the psalm, slowly, letting the words sink into our soul. Truly, God loves a sincere heart that is committed to Him. The slower and more intentionally the psalm is read increases the opportunity for personal transformation through *Canto Divina.* One might begin to hear certain words from the psalm calling out to them. This is the invitation from Jesus to dig deeper and learn from Him. Keeping a personal Bible close by and highlighting these words from the psalm can offer a wonderful connection to the reader. Our Bibles are our link to the love of God and can be accessed at any time of day or night.

In unity, we come together to sing the Psalm. We let the love of God connect our voices with the music and allow the Holy Spirit to come into our hearts. Relax, and rest in the assurance that God is with you. As you lift your voice in praise and thanksgiving to God, He will bless you abundantly. All voices are in tune when they are united with Christ.

Meditatio is a time to connect with God and let Him show you one phrase from the psalm. Be still and know. Wait for God to whisper in your ear or bring you a recurring thought. This is the sound of His voice. When a thought comes from God, you will be filled with peace. As you take this thought captive in your heart, allow God to show you how it pertains to your life today. He will reveal a person, place, or situation that He wants you to look at deeper. As you sort through different images, there will be one to which you keep coming back. This is the one to consider in the light of the words of the psalm.

As you reflect on this person, place, or situation, think about God's love and His desire to illuminate anything about your life that is holding you back from receiving His boundless love. I like to write out this meditation, as it helps me to let go of what was and invite God's light into revealing a new perspective to me. Yes, Jesus is the way, the truth, and the life. He who believes in him, will never die.

Oratio is a time to pray and invite God into your heart. It is time to ask, seek, and receive the love of God. This is a time to be open, honest, and direct with God and write Him your request letter. I like to start mine with, "Dear God, I love you, I need you, I adore you. Please help me." This act of humility and surrender to God's will in your life opens many doors to spiritual transformation. God sees and knows everything. When we ask for God's help to reveal His glory on earth to others through our life story, He blesses us abundantly. He loves every soul that turns to Him for help and grants them His favor if it is in accordance with His Divine Will.

Contemplatio is a time for God to answer us through Scripture. When we read and study the Bible, this becomes the language that God uses to communicate directly with us. As we turn to Him for answers, He reveals them to us in Scripture. If reading scripture is new for you, please take this time to open your Bible and ask God to reveal His answer to you. Sometimes, we simply open the Bible to a random page and start reading, and other times we are led to a particular Gospel. The words of the Bible are real and will enter your heart.

After several years of reading the Bible, the answers to my questions would come directly from God through Scripture. Many times, I have heard Him remind me of the words of Isaiah 54:10: "For the mountains may depart and the hills be removed, but my mercy shall not depart from you, and my covenant of peace shall not be removed, says the Lord, who has compassion on you." Jesus loves us so very much and only hopes to be in loving full communion with us each and every day. *Contemplatio* is a beautiful time to let the words of the psalm connect you to the words of the Gospels and be transformed. This happens best when we sit at the foot of the cross and surrender our lives to Him and listen.

Operatio is a time to apply the lessons we have learned from our transformation in Christ and put them into action. With a heart open to God, all things are possible. Allow God to show you how to implement this new thought, idea, or concept in your life to love and serve Him today. Each day that we offer our lives to be transformed into His image and likeness we are given detailed instructions on how to move forward with grace. Each day that we apply these new concepts we are helping to build the Body of Christ and bringing others into the Kingdom of God.

I offer you now my own personal examples of *Canto Divina* as a guide for your instruction. I have outlined the process of *Canto Divina* for your reference. Please see Appendix A for a list of additional music resources.

Canto Divina

Canto:
Choose a psalm. Listen to an authentic recording of the psalm. Read the psalm. Sing the psalm.
(Be open)

Meditatio:
Let the words of the psalm connect you to a person, place, or situation in your life.
(Reflect)

Oratio:
Pray to God for an answer to your reflection.
(Ask)

Contemplatio:
Allow God to speak to you through Scripture and be transformed in His image and likeness.
(Receive)

Operatio:
Ask God to show you one way to move forward in your life with this transformation.
(Act)

Psalm 16: Keep Me Safe, O God

Psalm 16
A Song of Trust and Security in God.
A Miktam of David.

Canto:

[1] Preserve me, O God,
For in you I take refuge.
[2] I say to the Lord, "You are my Lord;
I have no good apart from you.
[3] As for the saints in the land,
they are the noble,
in whom is all my delight.
[4] Those who choose another God
multiply their sorrows;
their libations of blood I will not pour out
or take their names upon my lips.
[5] The Lord is my chosen portion and my cup;
you hold my lot.
[6] The lines have fallen for me in pleasant places;
yes, I have a goodly heritage.
[7] I bless the Lord who gives me counsel;
in the night also my heart instructs me.
[8] I keep the Lord always before me;
because he is at my right hand,

I shall not be moved.
⁹ Therefore my heart is glad,
and my soul rejoices;
my body also dwells secure.
¹⁰ For you do not give me up to Sheol,
or let your godly one see the Pit.
¹¹ You show me the path of life;
in your presence there is fullness of joy,
in your right hand are pleasures for evermore.

Meditatio:
"You are my Lord; I have no good apart from you."

I was driving home from work along a winding country road
in New Hampshire on a Friday afternoon. It was mid-August,
and the weather was changing. I was field manager for a lovely
private homecare agency and thanking God for this opportunity to serve Him. It was raining on the drive home, and the
roads were slippery. Traffic was backed up on this two-lane
highway, and I glanced at the Bible sitting next to me in the
passenger seat. Suddenly, a strong wind came up and I heard a
loud crack. I was driving at about 20 mph, and a few yards off
to my right was an old tree with three large branches break-
ing off and heading in my direction. I looked before me and
behind me. I looked beside me. I was trapped. I looked beside
me and there was my Bible. I prayed. In the flash of a moment,
a twelve-foot branch that was shaped like a spear missed my
windshield and went straight through my radiator. My car was
totaled, and my life was spared. The difference between my life
and my death was 3 seconds. Truly, God had spared my life.
He protected me. You are my Lord; I have no good apart from
You.

Oratio:

Dear God,
Why me? Why did my car get hit by these three branches?
What am I doing wrong? What do I need to do? I am scared,
please help me. What do You want me to know and understand from this experience?

Contemplatio:

I can hear God reminding me that I can do nothing without
Him. Indeed His words come to me from John 15:5, "I am the
vine, you are the branches. He who abides in me, and I in him,
he it is that bears much fruit, for apart from me you can do
nothing."
  Life is not a solo flight. I recently had returned from
a year of traveling across the country conducting research on
music as medicine. I saw so many miracles happen in Alzheimer's patients as a direct result of music that I wanted to
understand how it worked so I could teach others how to apply
it to other health concerns. God showed me His power to heal
through the sound of His voice. He restored my vision while
singing "Hallelujah" during a parish healing mission. All glory
and honor to God, Our Savior! Yes, Lord, You are the vine,
and I am one of your branches. I am nothing without You.

Operatio:

I decided to attend daily Mass, so I would grow in commitment to my faith and build a strong community to support me
on this journey.

Psalm 22: My God, My God

Psalm 22
Plea for Deliverance from Suffering and Hostility.
To the choirmaster: according to "The Hind of the Dawn".
A Psalm of David.

Canto:

¹ My God, my God, why have you forsaken me?
Why are you so far from helping me, from the words of
my groaning?
² O my God, I cry by day, but you do not answer;
and by night, but find no rest.
³ Yet you are holy,
enthroned on the praises of Israel.
⁴ In you our fathers trusted;
they trusted, and you delivered them.
⁵ To you they cried, and were saved;
in you they trusted, and were not disappointed.
⁶ But I am a worm, and no man;
scorned by men, and despised by the people.
⁷ All who see me mock at me,
they make mouths at me,
they wag their heads;
⁸ "He committed his cause to the Lord;
let him deliver him,

let him rescue him, for he delights in him!"
⁹ Yet you are He who took me from the womb;
you kept me safe upon my mother's breasts.
¹⁰ Upon you was I cast from my birth,
and since my mother bore me
you have been my God.
¹¹ Be not far from me,
for trouble is near
and there is none to help.
¹² Many bulls encompass me,
strong bulls of Bashan surround me;
¹³ they open wide their mouths at me,
like a ravening and roaring lion.
¹⁴ I am poured out like water,
and all my bones are out of joint;
my heart is like wax,
it is melted within my breast;
¹⁵ my mouth is dried up like a potsherd,
and my tongue cleaves to my jaws;
you lay me in the dust of death.
¹⁶ Yes, dogs are round about me;
a company of evildoers encircle me;
they have pierced my hands and feet—
¹⁷ I can count all my bones—
they stare and gloat over me;
¹⁸ they divide my garments among them,
and for my clothing they cast lots.
¹⁹ But you, O Lord, be not far off!
O my help, hasten to my aid!
²⁰ Deliver my soul from the sword,
my life from the power of the dog!
²¹ Save me from the mouth of the lion,

my afflicted soul from the horns of the wild oxen!
[22] I will tell of your name to my brethren;
in the midst of the congregation I will praise you:
[23] You who fear the Lord, praise him!
all you sons of Jacob, glorify him,
and stand in awe of him,
all you sons of Israel!
[24] For he has not despised or abhorred the
affliction of the afflicted;
And he has not hidden his face from him,
but has heard, when he cried to him.
[25] From you comes my praise in the great
congregation;
my vows I will pay before those who fear him.
[26] The afflicted shall eat and be satisfied;
those who seek him shall praise the Lord!
May your hearts live for ever!
[27] All the ends of the earth shall remember
and turn to the Lord;
and all the families of the nations
shall worship before him.
[28] For dominion belongs to the Lord,
and he rules over the nations.
[29] Yes, to him shall all the proud of the earth bow
down;
before him shall bow all who go down to the dust,
and he who cannot keep himself alive.
[30] Posterity shall serve him;
men shall tell of the Lord to the coming generation,
[31] and proclaim his deliverance to a people yet
unborn,
that he has wrought it.

Meditatio:

"...let him deliver him, let him rescue him, for he delights in him!"

I completed my masters degree in social work with a focus on music as medicine. As a music educator I personally experienced and witnessed the power of music to heal. Music can reduce anxiety, relieve depression, and alleviate pain. Just think about David playing the harp for King Saul so long ago. Music works! God loves music! Indeed, music opens the door of our souls to the love of God. The Liturgy of the Eucharist also reminds us of the importance of sound in healing, "Only say the word, and my soul shall be healed." Yes, I had found my calling and was prepared to present my research at an important conference. The day before I was to leave for the conference, I became the victim of identity theft. I lost everything.

I remembered who I was, the royal daughter of a King, and I claimed my inheritance. I knelt at the foot of the statue of Saint Maximillian Kolbe in Marytown, Illinois, and I begged him to help me. In a moment I was filled with the gift of consolation, divine ecstasy, and the will to go forward. Jesus rescued me, and I found my way home with grace and strength.

Oratio:

Dear God,
Why me? Why did I have to lose everything to find You?

What do You want me to know? Or am I chosen to reveal You to others? Please, Lord...answer me.

Contemplatio:

I have always loved God, yet I struggle during times of stress to trust Him completely. There have been a few times in my life where there were many "dogs" encircling me. I paused and offered these times up to God and asked Him to show me what I needed to learn.

He reminded me of the Virgin Mary and her humble and trusting surrender to the will of God. In Luke 1:38 we read: "And Mary said, 'Behold, I am the handmaid of the Lord; let it be to me according to your word.' Then the angel departed from her."

Yes, humbly surrendering myself to the will and power of God to overcome any struggle in my life has blessed me abundantly.

Jesus is always victorious! He will deliver me and rescue me from my enemies.

Operatio:

I decided to become a lay Carmelite and read the Liturgy of the Hours each day. This helps me to remain humble and trusting in God at all times.

Psalm 23: The Lord Is My Shepherd

Psalm 23
The Divine Shepherd.
A Psalm of David.

Canto:

¹ The Lord is my shepherd, I shall not want;
² he makes me lie down in green pastures.
He leads me beside still waters;
³ he restores my soul.
He leads me in paths of righteousness
for his name's sake.
⁴ Even though I walk through the valley of the
shadow of death,
I fear no evil;
for you are with me;
your rod and your staff,
they comfort me.
⁵ You prepare a table before me
in the presence of my enemies;
you anoint my head with oil,
my cup overflows.
⁶ Surely goodness and mercy shall follow me
all the days of my life;
and I shall dwell in the house of the Lord
for ever.

Meditatio:

"You prepare a table before me in the presence of my enemies..."

Recovering from identity theft takes time. There were so many good Christian soldiers that stepped into this battle with me and invited me to the banquet of Christ. Jesus continued to bring me to His table in the presence of my enemies. Faithful servants continued to welcome me into their lives and sheltered me in the storm. Surely goodness and mercy followed me wherever I went.

As I continued to surrender my life to God and take one day at a time, I continued to move in the right direction. I offered this time of suffering in my life for the glory of God. I asked Jesus to guide me through this so that I could help others. Truly, His love is extravagant.

Oratio:

Dear God,
Why are so many people inviting me into their lives? Don't they know I have sinned against You? Why are they being so kind and hospitable? Don't they see and hear my enemies accusing me of things I have not done? Why do You love me so much to prepare a feast before my enemies?

Contemplatio:

Love and forgiveness walk hand in hand. I have met so many

lovely people all over the country who radiate the love and forgiveness of God in their words and actions. They all pointed me to the Eucharist. Jesus forgave His persecutors and found victory over sin and death. God was revealing His nature to me again. Those who love Him live a life of forgiveness. As it says in Luke 23:34: "Father, forgive them; for they know not what they do."

My home became the dwelling place of the Lord. Wherever I was He was with me. I detached myself from things of this world and embraced His love for me with complete abandon. Like clay in the potter's hands, I was becoming a new creation. I offered my life to reveal His glory to others. Each time I looked up into the sky and asked God if I was where He wanted me, the sun would come out and answer me with a hug from above. Yes, I was following Him. He had the answers.

Operatio:

As God began the restoration process in my life, I was abundantly blessed in every way. I decided to lead a life of forgiveness helping others along the way.

Psalm 25: To You, O Lord

Psalm 25
Prayer for Guidance and for Deliverance.
A Psalm of David.

Canto:

> [1] To you, O Lord, I lift up my soul.
> [2] O my God, in you I trust,
> let me not be put to shame;
> let not my enemies exult over me.
> [3] Yes, let none that wait for you be put to shame;
> let them be ashamed who
> are wantonly treacherous.
> [4] Make me know your ways, O Lord;
> teach me your paths.
> [5] Lead me in your truth, and teach me,
> for you are the God of my salvation;
> for you I wait all the day long.
> [6] Be mindful of your compassion, O Lord,
> and of your merciful love,
> for they have been from of old.
> [7] Remember not the sins of my youth, or my
> transgressions;
> according to your mercy remember me,
> for your goodness' sake, O Lord!

⁸ Good and upright is the Lord;
therefore he instructs sinners in the way.
⁹ He leads the humble in what is right,
and teaches the humble his way.
¹⁰ All the paths of the Lord are
mercy and faithfulness,
for those who keep his covenant and his testimonies.
¹¹ For your name's sake, O Lord,
pardon my guilt, for it is great.
¹² Who is the man that fears the Lord?
Him will he instruct in the way that he should choose.
¹³ He himself shall abide in prosperity,
and his children shall possess the land.
¹⁴ The friendship of the Lord is for those who fear
him,
and he makes known to them his covenant.
¹⁵ My eyes are ever toward the Lord,
for he will pluck my feet out of the net.
¹⁶ Turn to me, and be gracious to me;
for I am lonely and afflicted.
¹⁷ Relieve the troubles of my heart,
and bring me out of my distresses.
¹⁸ Consider my affliction and my trouble,
and forgive all my sins.
¹⁹ Consider how many are my foes,
and with what violent hatred they hate me.
²⁰ Oh, guard my life, and deliver me;
let me not be put to shame,
for I take refuge in you.
²¹ May integrity and uprightness preserve me,
for I wait for you.
²² Redeem Israel, O God, out of all his troubles.

Meditatio:

"He leads the humble in what is right..."

We live in a world of snapchats, photos, and instant messaging. Many people do not take the time to know or understand someone else truly, and they make snap decisions and judgments about others that are false.

When you lose everything, you find out who you really are. Your true identity as a son or daughter of Christ is revealed. Life changes. Knowing God as the Father, the Son, and the Holy Spirit is a divine awakening. He is my best friend, and I love Him with complete abandon. He knows I would do anything for Him, as He has done everything for me. I wake up every morning asking Him what He would like me to do for Him today. He answers me each day, one holy moment at a time.

Oratio:

Dear God,
I am so sorry I did not listen to You before. I am so sorry I hurt Your heart. I am so sorry I did not know any better at the time. God, why do You still love me? Why do You forgive me? Why do You give me another chance?

Contemplatio:

God answered me in Philippians 2:1-5:

> So if there is any encouragement in Christ, any incentive of love, any participation in the Spirit, any affection and sympathy, complete my joy by being of the same mind, having the same love, being in full accord and of one mind. Do nothing from selfishness or conceit, but in humility count others better than your selves. Let each of you look not only to his own inteests, but also to the interests of others. Have this mind among yourselves, which was in Christ Jesus...

Please, Lord, help me to regard others as better than myself. Lord, let me be Your servant. Lord, let me rise above the pain and forgive. Please Lord, let my life reveal You.

Operatio:

Lord, You have forgiven me my sins. I will forgive others their sins. Yes, I will choose a life of forgiveness and love.

Psalm 27: The Lord Is My Light

Psalm 27
Triumphant Song of Confidence.
A Psalm of David.

Canto:
    [1] The Lord is my light and my salvation;
whom shall I fear?
The Lord is the stronghold of my life;
of whom shall I be afraid?
    [2] When evildoers assail me
to devour my flesh,
my adversaries and foes,
they shall stumble and fall.
    [3] Though a host encamp against me,
my heart shall not fear;
though war rise up against me,
yet I will be confident.
    [4] One thing have I asked of the Lord,
that will I seek after;
that I may dwell in the house of the Lord
all the days of my life,
to behold the beauty of the Lord,
and to inquire in his temple.
    [5] For he will hide me in his shelter
in the day of trouble;

he will conceal me under the cover of his tent,
he will set me high upon a rock.
⁶ And now my head shall be lifted up
above my enemies round about me;
and I will offer in his tent
sacrifices with shouts of joy;
I will sing and make melody to the Lord.
⁷ Hear, O Lord, when I cry aloud,
be gracious to me and answer me!
⁸ You have said, "Seek my face."
My heart says to you,
"Your face, Lord, do I seek."
⁹ Hide not your face from me.
Turn not your servant away in anger,
you who have been my help.
Cast me not off, forsake me not,
O God of my salvation!
¹⁰ If my father and my mother
have forsaken me,
but the Lord will take me up.
¹¹ Teach me your way, O Lord;
and lead me on a level path
because of my enemies.
¹² Give me not up to the will of my adversaries;
for false witnesses have risen against me,
and they breathe out violence.
¹³ I believe that I shall see the
goodness of the Lord
in the land of the living!
¹⁴ Wait for the Lord;
be strong, and let your heart

take courage;
yes, wait for the Lord!

Meditatio:

"I believe that I shall see the goodness of the Lord in the land of the living!"

I had the pleasure of directing a vacation bible school program at Saint Pius X Parish in Appleton, Wisconsin. We used the Totally Catholic vacation bible school curriculum published by *Our Sunday Visitor*, which includes the *Sing and Play Roar* music published by Group Publishing Inc. To prepare the children, families, and staff to get the most out of our week together we gave *Sing and Play Roar* CDs to everyone upon registration. The parish blessed me during a difficult time in my life, and I wanted to give back to them. I chose our theme song to be "God is Good". No matter what our circumstances in life, if we trust in God, He will always come through for us!

By the end of our week together, the joy was contagious! Singing, dancing, and praising God as a community of Catholics dispelled all fear and united us as the Body of Christ.

Oratio:

Dear God,
Why can't we sing and dance like this each week in church?
How do I bring Your love and goodness to the children, to the families, to the parish? Please help me, Lord. I want them to know Your love and goodness 365 days a year.

Contemplatio:

God answered me in Romans 8:28: "We know that in everything God works for good with those who love him, who are called according to his purpose."

Yes, Lord, I will work together with the priests, teachers, families, and children to reveal Your love and goodness to them. Please remove any barriers between us so that You may be glorified.

Operatio:

I decided to integrate the concepts of the Totally Catholic VBS program into the children's Liturgy of the Word curriculum. The first half of the year would reinforce the concepts of the previous summer's VBS program, and the second half of the year would prepare the concepts for the next summer's VBS program. Once the curriculum was completed, I shared it with the parish team and communicated regularly with the parish families for feedback and development.

Lord, please let me be the light!

Psalm 30: I Will Extol You, O Lord

Psalm 30
Thanksgiving for Recovery from Grave Illness.
A Psalm of David.
A Song at the dedication of the Temple.

Canto:

¹ I will extol you, O Lord,
for you have drawn me up,
and have not let my foes rejoice over me.
² O Lord my God,
I cried to you for help,
and you have healed me.
³ O Lord, you have brought up
my soul from Sheol,
restored me to life from among those gone down
to the Pit.
⁴ Sing praises to the Lord,
O you his saints,
and give thanks to his holy name.
⁵ For his anger is but for a moment,
and his favor is for a lifetime.
Weeping may last for the night,
but joy comes with the morning.
⁶ As for me, I said in my prosperity,

"I shall never be moved."
⁷ By your favor, O Lord,
you had established me as a strong mountain;
you hid your face,
I was dismayed.
⁸ To you, O Lord, I cried;
and to the Lord I made supplication:
⁹ "What profit is there in my death,
if I go down to the Pit?
Will the dust praise you?
Will it tell of your faithfulness?
¹⁰ Hear, O Lord, and be gracious to me!
O Lord, be my helper!"
¹¹ You have turned my mourning into dancing;
you have loosed my sackcloth
and clothed me with gladness,
¹² that my soul may praise you and not be silent.
O Lord my God,
I will give thanks to you for ever.

Meditatio:

"I cried to you for help, and you have healed me."

I have always been drawn to the healing power of Christ. The
New Testament is filled with stories of miracles performed
by Jesus during His three-year public ministry.   None of the
prophets of the Old Testament or any of Christ's disciples
could claim healing power except as coming from God. Jesus,
on the other hand, is God, and He is the source from which all
healing comes. Jesus heals. My favorite childhood song says,

"I am the resurrection and the life, he who believes in me will live a new life." I believe in Jesus and the power of His Resurrection. It is that simple.

So, when the perfect storm hit in my life, and my energy levels were so depleted that my eyes could not focus properly, I cried out to Jesus for help: "Lord, for Your glory...please restore my vision. I have trifocals with prisms that are not working, and I can't afford another eye surgery. I can't find my way through this storm, but You can. I love You. I adore You. I believe in You. Please help me."

A few days later, Father Greg Bramlage, founder of the Missionaries of the New Evangelization, offered a parish healing mission at Saint Pius X in Appleton, Wisconsin. I had been blessed by the abundant programs of the New Evangelization upon my return to Catholicism, and my heart was open to this ministry. On the third night of the mission, while singing "Hallelujah", my vision was healed. My eyes were never able to focus together even after childhood strabismus surgery. In a holy moment, the Holy Spirit brought my left eye straight, and my eyes began working together. When I woke up the next morning, I could read without glasses. The following day I could drive without glasses. It has been one year since this healing of my vision began, and God is blessing me abundantly.

Oratio:

Dear God,
Why me? There are so many others that need healing from more serious afflictions. You have blessed me so much in my life with two beautiful children. I asked You for help, but I

never imagined You would perform a miracle in my life and restore my vision. Lord, what do You want me to do? How on earth do I say thank You?

Contemplatio:

The Lord answered me in Zephaniah 3:15: "The Lord has taken away the judgments against you, he has cast out your enemies. The King of Israel, the Lord, is in your midst; you shall fear evil no more."

Yes, Jesus is victorious! He loves to take care of widows and orphans. He never abandons anyone. He is a mighty King and Warrior! All glory be to God!

Operatio:

I decided to serve as a member of the missionary team for the Missionaries of the New Evangelization. Yes, the blind can see, the mute can hear, and the lame can walk.

Psalm 51: Create in Me a Clean Heart

Psalm 51
Prayer for Cleansing and Pardon
To the choirmaster
A Psalm of David, when Nathan the prophet came to him,
after he had gone in to Bathsheba.

Canto:

> [1] Have mercy on me, O God,
> according to your merciful love;
> according to your abundant mercy
> blot out my transgressions.
> [2] Wash me thoroughly from my iniquity,
> and cleanse me from my sin!
> [3] For I know my transgressions,
> and my sin is ever before me.
> [4] Against you, you only, have I sinned,
> and done that which is evil in your sight,
> so that you are justified in your sentence
> and blameless in your judgment.
> [5] Behold, I was brought forth in iniquity,
> and in sin did my mother conceive me.
> [6] Behold, you desire truth in the inward being;
> therefore teach me wisdom in my secret heart.
> [7] Purge me with hyssop, and I shall be clean;
> wash me, and I shall be whiter than snow.

⁸ Make me hear joy and gladness;
let the bones which you have broken rejoice.
⁹ Hide your face from my sins,
and blot out all my iniquities.
¹⁰ Create in me a clean heart, O God,
and put a new and right spirit within me.
¹¹ Cast me not away from your presence,
and take not your holy Spirit from me.
¹² Restore to me the joy of your salvation,
and uphold me with a willing spirit.
¹³ Then I will teach transgressors your ways,
and sinners will return to you.
¹⁴ Deliver me from bloodguilt, O God,
O God of my salvation,
and my tongue will sing aloud of your deliverance.
¹⁵ O Lord, open my lips,
and my mouth shall show forth your praise.
¹⁶ For you take no delight in sacrifice;
were I to give a burnt offering, you would not be
pleased.
¹⁷ The sacrifice acceptable to God is a broken
spirit;
a broken and contrite heart, O God,
you will not despise.
¹⁸ Do good to Zion in your good pleasure;
rebuild the walls of Jerusalem,
then you will delight in right sacrifices,
in burnt offerings and whole burnt offerings;
then bulls will be offered on your altar.

Meditatio:

"Wash me thoroughly from my iniquity, and cleanse me from my sin!"

God became completely real to me in the restoration of my vision. Any fears, doubts, or disbeliefs I held about Catholicism were washed away in an instant. Every word in the Bible came alive and made sense to me in a whole new way. God knew my heart, my mind, my body, and my soul. It was time to claim my baptism and purify my heart through the beautiful sacraments of our Church. I learned that our national shrines offer many additional graces not always found in our local churches. Father John Broussard, rector of the National Shrine of Our Lady of Good Help, became my spiritual director and guided me in the complete purification of my heart.

The gift of the sacrament of reconciliation is extraordinary! Truly, when we come to Jesus with an honest and humble heart, we receive His forgiveness and our sins are washed away. This opens our hearts to receive the abundant graces of God's love and mercy. We are a new creation!

Oratio:

Dear God,
I am so sorry for having sinned against You. I realize now how much my sins hurt Your heart. You are all loving and deserving of my love. Thank You for loving me so much. Please show me how I can help others find Your love and forgiveness.

Contemplatio:

God answered me in Zephaniah 3:19: "Behold, at that time I will deal with all your oppressors. And I will save the lame and gather the outcast, and I will change their shame into praise and renown in all the earth."

Yes, God promised to save the lame and gather the outcast and remove their shame. He will gather us together and bring us home to Him at just the right time.

Operatio:

I decided to begin training in healing and deliverance ministries. Unbound, Missionaries of the New Evangelization, and Transformational Prayer Ministry all led the way for my continued growth and development.

Psalm 91: He Will Give His Angels Charge of You

Psalm 91
Assurance of God's Protection.

Canto:

¹ He who dwells in the shelter of the Most High,
who abides in the shadow of the Almighty,
² will say to the Lord, "My refuge and my for
tress;
my God, in whom I trust."
³ For he will deliver you from the snare of the
fowler
and from the deadly pestilence;
⁴ he will cover you with his pinions,
and under his wings you will find refuge;
his faithfulness is a shield and buckler.
⁵ You will not fear the terror of the night,
nor the arrow that flies by day,
⁶ nor the pestilence that stalks in darkness,
nor the destruction that wastes at noonday.
⁷ A thousand may fall at your side,
ten thousand at your right hand;
but it will not come near you.
⁸ You will only look with your eyes
and see the recompense of the wicked.
⁹ Because you have made the Lord your refuge,

the Most High your habitation,
¹⁰ no evil shall befall you,
no scourge come near your tent.
¹¹ For he will give his angels charge of you
to guard you in all your ways.
¹² On their hands they will bear you up,
lest you dash your foot against a stone.
¹³ You will tread on the lion and the adder,
the young lion and the serpent
you will trample under foot.
¹⁴ Because he clings to me in
Love, I will deliver him;
I will protect him, because
he knows my name.
¹⁵ When he calls to me, I will answer him;
I will be with them in trouble,
I will rescue him and honor him.
¹⁶ With long life I will satisfy him,
and show him my salvation.

Meditatio:

"…and under his wings you will find refuge…"

I have always been drawn to the ethereal beauty of angel's wings. The complexity of their formation and the power of their unity fascinate me. Perhaps, the mystery of flight or rising above worldly things lies in the grace and strength of their formation. As they soar like eagles, riding on the wind, there is a freedom and beauty that calls to me. The first time I experienced the protection of God through His legions of angels occurred when I was singing over a prayer ministry supplicant to Julie True's recording of "Heavens Embrace".

It was my first experience as a Missionary of the New Evangelization with Father Greg Bramlage at Our Lady of Mount Carmel Parish in Maryland. I asked God for spiritual protection as I entered the realm of the Spirit to help others. Within a few minutes of singing along with the music as my hands were placed over the prayer supplicant's head, a choir of angels appeared over me with a doorway to heaven. A beautiful light poured out through me, and both Father Greg and the prayer ministry supplicant felt the angels present. Yes, anointed music opens the door to the healing love of Christ. The angels came to guide me, protect me, and teach me how to be the hands and feet of Christ on earth.

Oratio:

Dear God,
Why me? What is happening to me? What do You want of me? How will I ever live up to Your desires for my life? My life is no longer my own; yet it is more beautiful than I ever could have imagined. Please help me, Lord. Please keep me under the shadow of Your wings as I draw closer to You.

Contemplatio:

God answered me in Isaiah 54:17: "…no weapon that is fashioned against you shall prosper, and you shall confute every tongue that rises against you in judgment. This is the heritage of the servants of the Lord and their vindication from me, says the Lord."

Praise God! As I stepped into the world of spiritual warfare, God protected me. Just like David's faith while throwing the stone at Goliath, I had faith in God with His legions of angels to protect and provide for my every need.

Operatio:

I decided to learn more about the legions of angels and found this prayer to recite daily:

> *August Queen of Heaven, Sovereign Mistress of the Angels, thou, who from the beginning hast received from God the power of the mission to crush the head of Satan, we humbly implore thee, to send thy holy legions so that under thy command and by thy power, they may drive the devils away, every where, fight them, subduing their boldness and thrust them down into the abyss.*
>
> *Who is like unto God?*
>
> *O good and tender Mother, thou willst always be our love and our hope.*
>
> *O divine Mother, send Thy holy angels to defend me and drive far away from me the cruel enemy.*
>
> *Holy Angels and Archangels defend us, keep us. Amen.*

(Original text from the prayer dedicated by Our Lady to Blessed Father Louis-Édouard Louis Cestac on January 13, 1864)

Psalm 103: The Lord Is Kind and Merciful

Psalm 103
Thanksgiving for God's Goodness.
A Psalm of David.

Canto:

    [1] Bless the Lord, O my soul;
    and all that is within me,
    bless his holy name!
    [2] Bless the Lord, O my soul,
    and forget not all his benefits,
    [3] who forgives all your iniquity,
    who heals all your diseases,
    [4] who redeems your life from the Pit,
    who crowns you with mercy and compassion,
    [5] who satisfies you with good as long as you live
    so that your youth is renewed like the eagle's.
    [6] The Lord works vindication and justice for all
    who are oppressed.
    [7] He made known his ways to Moses,
    his acts to the people of Israel.
    [8] The Lord is merciful and gracious,
    slow to anger and abounding in mercy.
    [9] He will not always chide,
    nor will he keep his anger for ever.
    [10] He does not deal with us according to our sins,
    nor repay us according to our iniquities.

¹¹ For as the heavens are high above the earth,
so great is his mercy toward those who fear him;
¹² as far as the east is from the west,
so far does he remove our transgressions from us.
¹³ As a father pities his children,
so the Lord pities those who fear him.
¹⁴ For he knows our frame;
he remembers that we are dust.
¹⁵ As for man, his days are like grass;
he flourishes like a flower of the field;
¹⁶ for the wind passes over it, and it is gone,
and its place knows it no more.
¹⁷ But the mercy of the Lord is from everlasting
to everlasting
upon those who fear him,
and his righteousness to children's children,
¹⁸ to those who keep his covenant
and remember to do his commandments.
¹⁹ The Lord has established his throne in the
heavens,
and his kingdom rules over all.
²⁰ Bless the Lord, O you his angels,
you mighty ones who do his word,
hearkening to the voice of his word!
²¹ Bless the Lord, all his hosts,
his ministers that do his will!
²² Bless the Lord, all his works,
in all places of his dominion.
Bless the Lord, O my soul!

Meditatio:

"…who crowns you with mercy and compassion…"

It is very humbling to receive the mercy and compassion of Our Lord. We realize how small we are and how infinite He is. As my healing continued, Our Blessed Mother would come to me when I was in church and wrap her mantle around me: she was comforting me in the storm. A few months later, I felt her place a crown upon my head. I had no idea what she wanted of me but then, I read this psalm.

As I moved forward with serving Jesus, I would lead with mercy and compassion. Casting out all fear, blame, and judgment, I would bring others to the limitless love of Jesus with grace and forgiveness. I had walked in their footsteps and understood the suffering of being separated from God. I also understood God's desire to restore His relationship with each and every one of us. One step at a time, one person at a time, we would work together to rebuild the Kingdom of God here on earth.

Oratio:

Dear God,
Thank You for welcoming me into Your holy family. Thank You for bringing me Your mercy and compassion. Please show me what Your will is for my life. Please take away my sins. Our Blessed Mother, thank you for loving me and comforting me. Please show me how to lead with mercy and compassion.

Contemplatio:

God answered me in Deuteronomy 30:3: "…the Lord your God will restore your fortunes, and have compassion upon you, and he will gather you again from all the peoples where the Lord your God has scattered you."

In order to serve Our Lord, we need to have a community of loving Catholics who stand by us and pray for us at all times. God promised to restore every aspect of my life as I committed to serve Him. He knows everything that we need before we do, and He has a great plan to provide for us. Yes, Lord, I will listen and follow you.

Operatio:

I decided to say a rosary each night and include all the people I encountered that day in my intentions. I would offer each decade directly for a person in need.

Psalm 104: Lord, Send Out Your Spirit

Psalm 104
God the Creator and Provider.

Canto:

> ¹ Bless the Lord, O my soul!
> O Lord my God, you are very great!
> ² You are clothed with honor and majesty,
> who cover yourself with light as with a garment,
> who have stretched out the heavens like a tent,
> ³ who have laid the beams of your chambers on
> the waters,
> who make the clouds your chariot,
> who ride on the wings of the wind,
> ⁴ who make the winds your messengers,
> fire and flame your ministers.
> ⁵ You set the earth on its foundations,
> so that it should never be shaken.
> ⁶ You covered it with the deep as with a garment;
> the waters stood above the mountains.
> ⁷ At your rebuke they fled;
> at the sound of your thunder they took to flight.
> ⁸ The mountains rose, the valleys sank down
> to the place which you appointed for them.
> ⁹ You set a bound which they should not pass,

so that they might not again cover the earth.
¹⁰ You make springs gush forth in the valleys;
they flow between the hills,
¹¹ they give drink to every beast of the field;
the wild donkeys quench their thirst.
¹² By them the birds of the air have their habitation;
they sing among the branches.
¹³ From your lofty abode you water the mountains;
the earth is satisfied with the fruit of your work.
¹⁴ You cause the grass to grow for the cattle,
and plants for man to cultivate,
that he may bring forth food from the earth,
¹⁵ and wine to gladden the heart of man,
oil to make his face shine,
and bread to strengthen man's heart.
¹⁶ The trees of the Lord are watered abundantly,
the cedars of Lebanon which he planted.
¹⁷ In them the birds build their nests;
the stork has her home in the fir trees.
¹⁸ The high mountains are for the wild goats;
The rocks are a refuge for the badgers.
¹⁹ You have made the moon to mark the seasons;
The sun knows its time for setting.
²⁰ You make darkness, and it is night,
when all the beasts of the forest creep forth.
²¹ The young lions roar for their prey,
seeking their food from God.
²² When the sun rises, they get them away
and lie down in their dens.
²³ Man goes forth to his work
and to his labor until the evening.

^{24} O Lord, how manifold are your works!
In wisdom you have made them all;
the earth is full of your creatures.
^{25} Yonder is the sea, great and wide,
which teems with things innumerable,
living things both small and great.
^{26} There go the ships,
and Leviathan which you formed to sport in it.
^{27} These all look to you,
to give them their food in due season.
^{28} When you give to them, they gather it up;
when you open your hand, they are filled with good
things.
^{29} When you hide your face, they are dismayed;
when you take away their spirit,
they die and return to their dust.
^{30} When you send forth your Spirit, they are
created;
and you renew the face of the earth.
^{31} May the glory of the Lord endure for ever,
may the Lord rejoice in his works,
^{32} who looks on the earth and it trembles,
who touches the mountains and they smoke!
^{33} I will sing to the Lord as long as I live;
I will sing praise to my God while I have being.
^{34} May my meditation be pleasing to him,
for I rejoice in the Lord.
^{35} Let sinners be consumed from the earth,
and let the wicked be no more!
Bless the Lord, O my soul!
Praise the Lord!

Meditatio:

"I will sing to the Lord as long as I live…"

I have always enjoyed singing, especially Christian and sacred music! No matter what happened in my life, I always turned to the love of God as expressed in His music. I was fortunate enough to grow up by the water, and I enjoyed the sounds of God's creation as well as the psalms and hymns sung each week at Mass. It amazed me at times to think about the psalms being sung around the world each day-- by the trillions!

As much as I love to sing, I have also been drawn to playing the flute. When I play the flute, I am most focused on the air that I breathe. It is a contemplative practice in which I feel the love of God for His Son as expressed by the Holy Spirit. As God breathed the Holy Spirit on His Apostles, I know there is something unique about our breath. God's breath. When I played my flute at church, I prayed for God's love to come through the sound of my music and heal the faithful. When I played my flute in orchestras, bands, and choirs, I prayed for God to unify our sound and our souls to bring beauty to the earth.

Yes, singing and praising the Lord is essential to my health and well-being!

Oratio:

Dear God,
What is it about music that draws me close to You? When I close my eyes and listen to the sound of Your voice, I am completely filled with Your love. When I sing Your praises, it

is as if we are one. When I hear the Benedictine nuns singing Gregorian Chant, I sense that I am as close to heaven as I can be here on earth. Lord, please help me understand how You heal through music. Is it the Scripture being sung? Is it the sound of the voice singing? Or is it the ear hearing the music? Or perhaps, all three working together?

Contemplatio:

God answered me in Psalm 150:6 : "Let everything that breathes praise the Lord!" When we open our hearts to God and we allow His love to flow in and through us, we are abundantly blessed. We are loved, we are healed, we are made new. We praise Him for his mighty deeds and surpassing greatness! We praise Him with trumpets, lutes, harps, tambourines, flutes, strings, and cymbals! God just wants to love us!

When we receive His love, all we can do is love, adore, and praise Him. Perhaps this act of gratitude through music reaches God's heart most? I love to think of heaven as choirs and orchestras of angels singing and playing music for Our Lord!

Operatio:

I decided to make a recording of me performing these psalms to help bring Christ closer to us.
All glory be to God!

Psalm 116: I Will Walk with the Lord

Psalm 116
Thanksgiving for Recovery from Illness.

Canto:

> [1] I love the Lord, because he has heard
> my voice and my supplications.
> [2] Because he inclined his ear to me,
> therefore I will call on him as long as I live.
> [3] The snares of death encompassed me;
> the pangs of Sheol laid hold on me;
> I suffered distress and anguish.
> [4] Then I called on the name of the Lord:
> "O Lord, I beg you, save my life!"
> [5] Gracious is the Lord, and righteous;
> our God is merciful.
> [6] The Lord preserves the simple;
> when I was brought low, he saved me.
> [7] Return, O my soul, to your rest;
> for the Lord has dealt bountifully with you.
> [8] For you have delivered my soul from death,
> my eyes from tears,
> my feet from stumbling;
> [9]   I will walk before the Lord
> in the land of the living.

[10] I kept my faith, even when I said,
"I am greatly afflicted";
[12] I said in my consternation,
"Men are all a vain hope."
[12] What shall I render to the Lord
for all his bounty to me?
[13] I will lift up the chalice of salvation
and call on the name of the Lord,
[14] I will pay my vows to the Lord
in the presence of all his people.
[15] Precious in the sight of the Lord
is the death of his saints.
[16] O Lord, I am your servant;
I am your servant, the son of your handmaid.
You have loosed my bonds.
[17] I will offer to you the sacrifice of
thanksgiving
and call on the name of the Lord.
[18] I will pay my vows to the Lord
in the presence of all his people,
[19] in the courts of the house of the Lord,
in your midst, O Jerusalem.
Praise the Lord!

Meditatio:

"The Lord preserves the simple…"

One of the ways I have coped with difficult transitions in my life is to offer a daily walk of gratitude to Our Lord. The rhythm of my steps match the response, "Thank you, Jesus for…" This is not a complicated action, simply an offering of praise and thanksgiving.

The rest of my prayer life is also simple. I say a rosary each morning and intentionally offer prayers for my loved ones with each decade. At 3:00 pm, I offer a Divine Mercy Chaplet for the conversion of sinners. I finish my day with evening prayer and night prayer from the Divine Office.

My mind can handle complex information because my heart is simple. I love God. I listen to Him. I follow Him. Whatever I need to know, He shares with me when I need to know it. He has preserved my life, and I am grateful.

Oratio:

Dear God,
Why do You love me so much? Why do You answer me so clearly? Why have You preserved my life? How can I possible thank You enough?

Contemplatio:

The Lord answered me in the Song of Solomon 2:16: "My beloved is mine and I am his…" God is love. The Bible is a love story of God's creation, provision, healing, and restoration of His people. Perhaps the story of my life is about surrendering to the limitless love of God so that I can reveal the nature of His love to others.

Operatio:

I remembered the greatest commandment from Matthew 22:37-40:

> And he said to him, 'You shall love the Lord your God with all your heart, and with all your soul, and with all your mind. This is the greatest and first commandment. And a second is like it, You shall love your neighbor as yourself. On these two commandments depend all the law and the prophets.'

I decided to find more time in my day for helping my neighbors. I found the Lord and loved Him dearly, and now it is time to bring His love to others.

Psalm 118: Give Thanks to the Lord

Psalm 118
A Song of Victory.

Canto:

[20] O give thanks to the Lord,
for he is good;
his mercy endures for ever!
[21] Let Israel say,
"His mercy endures for ever."
[22] Let the house of Aaron say,
"His mercy endures for ever."
[23] Let those who fear the Lord say,
"His mercy endures for ever."
[24] Out of my distress I called on the Lord;
the Lord answered me and set me free.
[25] With the Lord on my side I do not fear.
What can man do to me?
[26] The Lord is on my side to help me;
I shall look in triumph on those who hate me.
[27] It is better to take refuge in the Lord
than to put confidence in man.
[28] It is better to take refuge in the Lord
than to put confidence in princes.
[29] All nations surrounded me;
in the name of the Lord I cut them off!

³⁰ They surrounded me, surrounded me on every
side;
in the name of the Lord I cut them off!
³¹ They surrounded me like bees,
they blazed like a fire of thorns;
in the name of the Lord I cut them off!
³² I was pushed hard, so that I was falling,
but the Lord helped me.
³³ The Lord is my strength and my song;
he has become my salvation.
³⁴ Listen, glad songs of victory
in the tents of the righteous:
"The right hand of the Lord does valiantly!
³⁵ The right hand of the Lord is exalted;
the right hand of the Lord does valiantly!"
³⁶ I shall not die, but I shall live,
and recount the deeds of the Lord.
³⁷ The Lord has chastened me sorely,
but he has not given me over to death.
³⁸ Open to me the gates of righteousness,
that I may enter through them
and give thanks to the Lord.
³⁹ This is the gate of the Lord;
the righteous shall enter through it.
⁴⁰ I thank you that you have answered me
and have become my salvation.
⁴¹ The stone which the builders rejected
has become the cornerstone.
⁴² This is the Lord's doing;
it is marvelous in our eyes.
⁴³ This is the day which the Lord has made;

let us rejoice and be glad in it.
⁴⁴ Save us, we beg you, O Lord!
O Lord, we beg you, give us success!
⁴⁵ Blessed be he who enters in the name of the Lord!
We bless you from the house of the Lord.
⁴⁶ The Lord is God,
and he has given us light.
Bind the festal procession with branches,
up to the horns of the altar!
⁴⁷ You are my God, and I will give thanks to you;
you are my God, I will extol you.
⁴⁸ O give thanks to the Lord, for he is good;
for his mercy endures for ever!

Meditatio:

"His mercy endures for ever."

I did not know that my conception had been blessed with
holy water from Our Lady of Lourdes until I interviewed my
mother for a graduate school assignment. Indeed, as an infant
she called me the "miracle child" because my parents had been
infertile for the previous fifteen years. I often wondered why
I seemed to overcome many obstacles in my life with a grace
that I would never fully understand. I was blessed with a grace
of forgiveness deep in my soul.

When I experienced any harm done, within a short
period of time I rose above and forgave the sinner. There have
been a few deeper wounds that took more time to forgive, but
ultimately I forgave. This enabled me to continue to love others even when they were not loving towards me.

Unfortunately, I was not as able to forgive myself. I struggled with self-forgiveness until I faced the mountain of fear that had crept into my life and found the mercy of God that endures forever. Once I tasted this gift of mercy, I understood the love of God even more and knew He would love me forever. My spiritual director guided me to understand that one of the greatest challenges in life is to accept the love of God. Once I did, my life was no longer my own. All glory be to God.

Oratio:

Dear God,
Why did I struggle so long with understanding Your mercy for me, a poor sinner? Why did You fill me with the grace to forgive others and I didn't accept it for myself? Why do You never give up on us?

Contemplatio:

God answered me in Mathew 18:21-22:

> Then Peter came and said to him, 'Lord, how often shall my brother sin against me, and I forgive him? As many as seven times?' Jesus said to him, 'I do not say to you seven times, but seventy times seven.'

I came to understand that forgiveness for both self and neighbor is essential to our Christian life.

When we understand that God sees everything and is the just judge, then we can let go of any bitterness, anger, or resentment and forgive. We can love ourselves and our neighbors as God loves us...completely and without abandon. We can trust the consequences of sin to the courts of heaven and lead with love and mercy.

Operatio:

I decided to kneel before Our Lord each time I received the Eucharist and ask forgiveness for my sins and the sins of others.

Psalm 146: Praise the Lord, My Soul

Psalm 146
Praise for God's Help.

Canto:

[49] Praise the Lord!
Praise the Lord, O my soul!
[50] I will praise the Lord as long as I live;
I will sing praises to my God while I have being.
[51] Put not your trust in princes,
in a son of man, in whom there is no help.
[52] When his breath departs he returns to his earth;
on that very day his plans perish.
[53] Happy is he whose help is the God of Jacob,
whose hope is in the Lord his God,
[54] who made heaven and earth,
the sea, and all that is in them;
who keeps faith for ever;
[55] who executes justice for the oppressed;
who gives food to the hungry.
The Lord sets the prisoners free;
[56] The Lord opens the eyes of the blind.
The Lord lifts up those who are bowed down;
the Lord loves the righteous.
[57] The Lord watches over the sojourners,

he upholds the widow and the fatherless;
but the way of the wicked he brings to ruin.
[58] The Lord will reign for ever,
your God, O Zion, to all generations.
Praise the Lord!

Meditatio:

"I will praise the Lord as long as I live…"

As my vision gradually was restored, I was overwhelmed with gratitude. In order to give back to Father Greg Bramlage and the Missionaries of the New Evangelization, I served on the next two parish missions in Maryland. While training as a missionary, I began singing to Julie True's "Heaven's Embrace" while praying over a supplicant. Within moments, a door to heaven opened and a canopy of angels appeared above us. Father Greg Bramlage guided my hands to settle on the supplicant's head, and we were all blessed with their presence.

Oratio:

Dear God,
What do I do now? What is happening to me? My life is not my own anymore, and I am afraid. Lord, please help me to follow You and have courage. I do not want to be separated from You ever again. Lord, my life is in Your hands.

Contemplatio:

God answered me in Psalm 149:1: "Praise the Lord! Sing to the Lord a new song, his praise in the assembly of the faithful!"

My life would now be a new song of praise and thanksgiving to Our Lord. It was that simple.

Operatio:

I decided to consecrate myself and my family to the Sacred Heart of Jesus and the Immaculate Heart of Mary. Together, we would join the Holy Family in love and mercy while serving others.

References

Angelica, Mother. *Mother Angelica on God, His Home, and His Angels.* EWTN Publishing, Inc., 2018, pp. 73–75.

Aquilina, Mike. *How the Choir Converted the World: Through Hymns, With Hymns, and In Hymns.* Emmaus Road Publishing, 2016.

Bach Cantatas Website. 2008. https://www.bach-cantatas.com/Lib/Palestrina.htm

Beck, R.J., T.C. Cesario, A. Yousefi, and H. Enamoto. "Choral singing, performance perception, and immune system changes in salivary immunoglobulin A and cortisol." Music Perception 18, no. 1 (1999): 87-106.

Bonilha, Amanda Gimenes, Fernando Onofre, Maria Lucia Vieira, Maria Yuka almeida Prado, and Jose Atonio Baddini Martinez. "Effects of singing classes on pulmonary function and quality of life of COPD patients." International Journal of COPD 4, (2009): 1-8.

Chorus America. "The chorus impact study: How children, adults, and communities benefit from choruses." Retrieved November 17, 2011 from the Chorus America website at https://www.chorusamerica.org/sites/default/files/resources/ImpactStudy09_Report.pdf

Clift, Stephen, & Grenville Hancox. "The perceived benefits of singing: Findings from preliminary Surveys of a university college choral society." Journal of the Royal Society for the Promotion of Health 121, no. 4 (2001): 248-256.

Clift, Stephen, Grenville Hancox, Rosalia Staricoff, & Christine Whitmore. "Singing and health: A systematic mapping and review of non-clinical research." Canterbury: Canterbury Christ Church University, 2008. Retrieved November 10, 2011 from http:///www.canterbury.ac.uk/centres/sidney-de-haan-research.

Clift, Stephen & Grenville Hancox. "The significance of choral singing for sustaining psychological well-being: Findings from a survey of choristers in England, Australia, and Germany." Music Performance Research 3, no. 1 (2010): 79-96.

Druart, Therese-Anne, "al-Farabi", The Stanford Encyclopedia of Philosophy (Fall 2020 edition), Edward N. Zalta (ed.),<https://plato.stanford.edu/archives/fall2020/entries/al-farabi/>.

Goodwin, Chris. 2001. "A Brief Introduction to the Lute." The Lute Society. https://www.lutesociety.org/pages/about-the-lute.

Henry, Hugh. "Veni Sancte Spiritus Et Emitte Coelitus." The Catholic Encyclopedia. Vol. 15. New York: Robert Appleton Company, 1912. 20 Oct. 2020 <http://www.newadvent.org/cathen/15342a.htm>.

Kleisiaris, Christos F. Chrisanthos Sfakianakis, & Ioanna V. Papathanasiou. 2014. "Health care practices in ancient Greece: The Hippocratic ideal." Journal of Medical Ethics and History of Medicine. 7: 6.

Kreutz, Gunter, Stephan Bongard, Sonja Rohrmann, Dorothee Grebe, H.G. Bastian, & Volker Hodapp. "Effects of choir singing or listening on secretory immunoglob ulin A, cortisol and emotional state." Journal of Behavioral Medicine 27, no. 6 (2004): 623-635.

Mansfield, Patti Gallagher. 1992. As by a New Pentecost: The Dramatic Beginning of the Catholic Charismatic Renewal. Steubenville: Franciscan University Press.

Murphy, John Joseph. 2011. Leading with Passion: 10 Essentials for Inspiring Others. Naperville: Simple Truths.

Appendix A: Musical Resources

The Psalms Project
From their website thepsalmsproject.com: "The Psalms Project is a band setting all 150 Psalms to music in their entirety, including the essential meaning of every verse, a marriage of King David's vision with modern worship music."

The Neumz Project
From their website neumz.com: "The entire Gregorian chant repertory, recorded by the community of Benedictine nuns of the Abbey of Notre-Dame de Fidélité of Jouques, in French Provence."

The Sons of Korah
From their website sonsofkorah.com: "Sons of Korah is an Australian based band devoted to giving a fresh voice to the biblical psalms. The Psalms have been the primary source for the worship traditions of both Judaism and Christianity going right back to ancient times."

Suggested Reading

Aquilina, Mike. *How the Choir Converted the World: Through Hymns, With Hymns, and In Hymns.* Emmaus Road Publishing, 2016.

Campbell, Don. (2001). *The Mozart Effect: Tapping the Power of Music to Heal the Body, Strengthen the Mind, and Unlock the Creative Spirit.* New York: HarperCollins Publishers, 2009.

Campell, Don and Alex Doman. *Healing at the Speed of Sound: How What We Hear Transforms Our Brains and Our Lives.* New York: Hudson Street Press, 2011.

Leeds, Joshua. *The Power of Sound: How to Be Healthy and Productive Using Music and Sound.* Rochester: Healing Arts Press, 2010.

Saunders, Laura I. *Your Brain on Music: The Cognitive Effects of Music Education on the Brain.* Higher Purpose Publishing, 2017.

Wong, Dr. Lisa with Robert Viagas. *Scales to Scalpels: Doctors Who Practice the Healing Arts of Music and Medicine.* New York: Pegasus Books, 2012.

About the Author

Deborah Ann Keefe, MSW offers *Canto Divina: Singing Psalms for Transformation* as a "Thank YOU" to God for the personal transformation she has experienced through sacred music, the holy sacraments, and the baptism of the Holy Spirit. After completing a nationwide research sabbatical on the application of music as medicine, she offers this work as an educator, author, and speaker. Deborah is abundantly blessed with two daughters and resides in the Pittsburgh area.

If you're interested in contacting Deborah
to come to your area for
training, seminars, speaking engagements, and consultations
— either in-person or online—
she can be reached at
cantodivina@gmail.com.

As an accomplished flautist, Deborah performed with the Cape Ann Symphony Orchestra, the Gordon College Flute Choir, and the New Hampshire Philharmonic Orchestra. Her flute teachers include Kathy Curran, Allison Loddengard, Heather Kent, Peter Bloom, and Kris Krueger. After witnessing the health and wellness benefits of music as a performer and educator, she completed her master's degree in social work at the University of New Hampshire in 2014 with a focus on the application of music as medicine.

Synopsis of Canto Divina

Canto Divina: Singing Psalms for Transformation is based upon the process of Lectio Divina and adds the gift of sacred music and the baptism of the holy spirit for transformation. This work strategically develops the research on music and medicine and the connection to Catholicism. Deborah presents her education, experience, and personal transformation through the music of our faith and supports this information with a summary of the history and science of music and medicine. The process of *Canto Divina* is then defined and practiced with appropriate examples to model this transformation. The psalms were chosen for this process of transformation as they clearly reflect the emotional connection to the heart of God through the words of King David. In this work the research and application of music and medicine has been fully integrated with Catholicism while providing a new intervention for transformation. As St. Augustine once noted, when we sing, we pray twice.

CPSIA information can be obtained
at www.ICGtesting.com
Printed in the USA
LVHW051639010623
748580LV00003B/465